D1220257

SIDEBROW BOOKS

THE VOLTA BOOK OF POETS

Published by Sidebrow Books
P.O. Box 86921
Portland, OR 97286
sidebrow@sidebrow.net
www.sidebrow.net

Cover art by Mark Warren Jacques and Meryl Pataky
Cover & book design by Jason Snyder

ISBN: 1-940090-01-6
ISBN-13: 978-1-940090-01-6

FIRST EDITION | FIRST PRINTING
9 8 7 6 5 4 3 2 1
SIDEBROW BOOKS 012
PRINTED IN THE UNITED STATES

Sidebrow Books titles are distributed by
Small Press Distribution

Titles are available directly from Sidebrow at
www.sidebrow.net/books

Funding for *The Volta Book of Poets* was made in large part by donations
to our Indiegogo campaign. Our sincerest gratitude to the 80 donors who
contributed, with special thanks to Matthew McGlincy. This book would
not have been possible without the community's generous support.

A Member of

Sidebrow is a member of the Intersection Incubator, a program of Intersection
for the Arts (www.theintersection.org) providing fiscal sponsorship, incubation,
and consulting for artists. Contributions to Sidebrow are tax-deductible to the
extent allowed by law.

THE VOLTA BOOK OF POETS

EDITED BY JOSHUA MARIE WILKINSON

INTRODUCTION BY JOSHUA MARIE WILKINSON i

ROSA ALCALÁ 1

ERIC BAUS 9

ANSELM BERRIGAN 17

EDMUND BERRIGAN 23

SUSAN BRIANTE 29

SOMMER BROWNING 37

JULIE CARR 43

DON MEE CHOI 51

ARDA COLLINS 59

DOT DEVOTA 67

TSERING WANGMO DHOMPA 75

GRAHAM FOUST 81

C.S. GISCOMBE 89

RENEE GLADMAN 97

NOAH ELI GORDON 105

YONA HARVEY 111

MATTHEW HENRIKSEN 117

HARMONY HOLIDAY 123

CATHY PARK HONG 129

BHANU KAPIL 135

JOHN KEENE 141

AARON KUNIN 149

DOROTHEA LASKY 157

JULIANA LESLIE 165

RACHEL LEVITSKY 171

TAN LIN 175

183 DAWN LUNDY MARTIN

191 J. MICHAEL MARTINEZ

197 FARID MATUK

203 SHANE McCRAE

209 ANNA MOSCHOVAKIS

217 FRED MOTEN

223 SAWAKO NAKAYASU

231 CHRIS NEALON

239 HOA NGUYEN

247 KHADIJAH QUEEN

253 ANDREA REXILIUS

259 ZACHARY SCHOMBURG

265 BRANDON SHIMODA

273 EVIE SHOCKLEY

281 CEDAR SIGO

289 ABRAHAM SMITH

297 CHRISTOPHER STACKHOUSE

303 MATHIAS SVALINA

309 ROBERTO TEJADA

315 TC TOLBERT

323 CATHERINE WAGNER

331 DANA WARD

339 RONALDO V. WILSON

347 LYNN XU

354 THE POETS

362 PERMISSIONS

INTRODUCTION

My goal in gathering poems for this anthology began as a relatively modest one: to cite a constellation of what is being written today by poets whose work I love. Anybody familiar with poetry is readily stunned by the sheer number of poets currently writing and publishing. But for those unfamiliar with poetry, finding a place to start can be intimidating to say the least. I work at a large public university, so I encounter the curious-yet-uninitiated by the dozens: who to read, where to begin, what websites and journals to follow—let alone what to value and why to value it—all become very tricky questions indeed. It's hardly a failing of theirs, or ours, as educators; whether you think of it as glut or a golden age of poetry, it's pretty cacophonous out there. Named for The Volta—an online journal and archive for poetry and poetics I continue to run—this anthology aims, in part, to embrace that cacophony and aid anyone looking to get acquainted with an unusual mix of poets writing today.

In the pages that follow, you will find poets of disparate backgrounds and traditions working in contrasting styles, utilizing forms inassimilable as a group or school. Poetry in its dissimilar pleasures, methods, and weirdnesses. Poets whose writing disarms and bewilders me. Poems that expand what a poem can say and do. Poetry that "resists the intelligence / Almost successfully," as Wallace Stevens famously said, or, as Tomaž Šalamun put it somewhere, "poems that impassionate me." And, in fact, some writers in this book blur the boundaries of what even gets called poetry.

The curious problem I encountered in curating this anthology was narrowing it down to just fifty poets, which had sounded like plenty for a compact, teachable book that wouldn't just become a doorstop. I still barely scratched the surface of what I believe should be read urgently. Consider this just some of the poets whose work I think anyone interested in poetry should get hooked on.

For Cole Swensen, reflecting on *American Hybrid: A Norton Anthology of New Poetry*, which she edited with David St. John, and responding elegantly to its myriad critics, "To ask an anthology to be inclusive of an entire moment in a culture as large and varied as that of the U.S. is, I think, unrealistic and unwise. For one, it's an impossible task." And Ron Silliman, discussing the latest edition of *Postmodern American Poetry: A Norton Anthology*, edited by Paul Hoover, takes this a little further: "It is no longer possible—not even plausible really—for the codex format to represent American or English language poetry in any depth whatsoever."

With so many anthologies defined by likeness (and I can think of many I love), I wondered whether showcasing difference would be a meaningful approach to this impossibility. As Mark Wallace has pointed out, "even if there were poetry anthologies that highlighted, rather than attempting to minimize or avoid, differences across groups, those anthologies would create not a new center but just another way of thinking." Indeed, this anthology represents an attempt to do just that: to present difference as a means for inspiring a new way to think about poetry, and to inspire new readership not just for the poets included, but for the myriad poetry communities and presses that embrace and publish them.

It's been a gift to work with Sidebrow Books—Jason, Kris, and John—on this project. The aesthetics of their first anthology, the range of their printed works are singular to me—because they produce the kinds of muddy, overlapping, and dissonant engagements as publishers that I've loved for a long while now. I remain their biggest fan and thank them for all their help and patience and brains. I'm grateful to all the poets included; I thank them for their diligence, their poems, their poetics, their wisdom and advice, and for helping me work with their myriad small and big presses to make this an affordable and doable endeavor.

Now, to the presses and publishers and editors and staff and assistants and permissions mavens and interns who helped us out: I am in your eternal debt. Your generosity and help and kindnesses in this process were totally stupefying and I thank you all. Really, it heartened me like nothing else. As a small press poet, as a small press editor and publisher myself, I was floored, nonetheless, that every single press we contacted was kind enough to work with us on this project, including: 1913 Press; Action Books; Ahsahta Press; Apogee Press; Birds, LLC; Black Lawrence Press; Black Ocean; Black Square Editions; City Lights Publishing; Cleveland State University Poetry Center; Counterpath Press; Dalkey Archive; Dorothy, a Publishing Project; Edge Books; Farfalla Press / McMillan; Fence Books; Flood Editions; Four Way Books; Futurepoem Books; Kenning Editions; Letter Machine Editions; Litmus Press; Noemi Press; Octopus Books; Omnidawn Publishing; Owl Press; W.W. Norton; and Wave Books. For my money, this list, in and of itself, is a pretty good starter map—radiating out to poets, books, journals, reading series, nonprofits, and other organizations—of what's happening in American poetry communities right now. To all of you: thank you.

—JMW, Tucson, Ariz.

This book is dedicated to Georgia & Gianna:

Once upon a time, your parents were pretty fucking cool

THE VOLTA BOOK OF POETS

ROSA ALCALÁ

"It is the activity of the voice on which the poem depends."

—Barbara Guest

"Voice is all that can cut through it."

—Alice Notley

"As I speak to you in English I think / translation is possible because /
thoughts are word less / and the voice is the transfiguration / of milk /
the milk of thought"

—Cecilia Vicuña

An article in *Time* magazine on voice activation technology discusses the failure of this innovation to recognize female or "foreign" voices with thick accents. Even a British-made car—programmed like everything else to comprehend a kind of American accent—responds to its British owner's commands with, "Sorry?" I sometimes worry that the ways in which we define poetry and separate it into exclusionary camps is like creating a technology that recognizes only a few representative voices—or no voice at all—and can only accomplish a limited set of commands. And like the British car, it seems to me that when we limit the recognition of voices to a few standardized ones, we also run the risk of creating a system that turns on us and refuses to recognize our own. The good news—what keeps people from dying in the poetry wars every day—is that poetry cannot be systematized and resists this kind of standardization, these definitions, and continues to grow in wild fields beyond the encampments we call "mainstream" and "experimental." There's no doubt that voice activation technology and its failures are only a reflection of society's ongoing inability to hear and encourage variance and complexity. I'm sure that my own voices—the mundane, as well as poetic ones—must be by now manufactured for recognition by someone. Even what might be called an "authentic voice" must be recognizable as such. What's remarkable about poetry, however, is that it pushes you—if you are not trapped by the sound of your own voice—to go off road. The poet's voice may activate the poem, but then the poem acquires, through this activation, it's own voice. If we are lucky, we are surprised by what we hear. Going off road may not be great for a driver who relies on his GPS to get to the emergency room, but it is necessary for the vitality of poetry—and for our own. Poetry even does things when the poet's voice is inaudible, garbled, incoherent, heavily accented, multilingual, etc. Especially when it is. I think my less successful poems have been those where I've turned off the poem's ability to speak and do for itself, and instead tried to translate, to make sense of my own incoherence—to make it do what I wanted it to do. Perhaps we all feel at times the need to control the message, to be clearly understood, especially if we've had mothers whose voices could only be heard through our own. "What does writing have to do with our mothers?" Susan Gervitz writes. For me, everything. It is the place from which my voice—and the poems it activates—departs, then multiplies. Returning and splitting, again and again.

VOICE ACTIVATION

"Do not forget that a poem, although it is composed in the language of information, is not used in the language-game of giving information."

—Ludwig Wittgenstein, *Zettel*

This poem, on the other hand, is activated by the sound of my voice, and, luckily, I am a native speaker. Luckily, I have no accent and you can understand perfectly what I am saying to you via this poem. I have been working on this limpid voice, from which you can read each word as if rounded in my mouth, as if my tongue were pushing into my teeth, my lips meeting and jaws flexing, so that even if from birth you've been taught to read faces before words and words as faces, you'll feel not at all confused with what I say on the page. But maybe you'll see my name and feel a twinge of confusion. Have no doubt, my poem is innocent and transparent. So when I say, I think I'll make myself a sandwich, the poem does not say, I drink an isle of bad trips. Or if I say, my mother is dying, where is her phone. The poem does not say, try other it spying, spare us ur-foam. One way to ensure the poem and its reader no misunderstanding is to never modulate. I'm done with emotion, I'm done, especially, with that certain weakness called exiting one's intention. What I mean is Spanish. What a mess that is, fishing for good old American bread, and ending up with a boatload of uncles and their boxes of salt cod, a round of aunts poking for fat in your middle. So you see, Wittgenstein, even the sandwich isn't always made to my specifications; it's the poem that does what I demand. Everything else requires a series of steps. I call the nurse's station and explain to the nurse—her accent thick as thieves—that I'd like to speak to my mother. She calls out to my mother: "it's your daughter" (really, she says this in Spanish, but for the sake of voice-activation and this poem, you understand I can't go there), and she hands the phone to my mother and my mother, who is not the poem, has trouble understanding me. So I write this poem, which understands me perfectly, and never needs the nurse's station, and never worries about unintelligible accents or speaking loudly enough or the trouble with dying, which can be understood as a loss of language. If so, the immigrant, my mother, has been misunderstood for so long, this death is from her last interpreters.

ARCHAEOLOGY OF VESTMENTS

I remember the fine pleats of your tunic, how they found you among the funerary rags. Your bicep, evident. The crease of your inner elbow. The perfect press that flattened each fold; a funny lie. You were wayward, you wallowed.

I remember pouring buckets of hot water onto ice until your body emerged. That you were preserved in your string skirt, hung low on the hips. Something alkaline made the threads rich, something made you kin.

I remember what you wore when there are now only words.

I remember how they chased you out of town in your own confection. A print unsuitable for marriage.

You wove and unwove, but you were no Penelope. You were my mother re-inventing English in her copy-cat fashion, and then you were a boy in a rock band whose ripped jeans I sold. And then you were a rack of babies, from which I stole one.

TRAINING

To each train its compartments, to each man his foiled sandwich.
Typically of ham or Spanish omelet. Things that keep their seats,
as assignments.

What is your first memory of jealous lovers? Were you yourself suspicious
of others? Here they are as I remember them. My daughter nurses the tally:

My brother puts a hand through a door inches from Farah Fawcett's stiletto.
My best friend writes an angry letter to her sister's boyfriend
      She later calls me out, accusing me of treason. I become her twin
              often out of convenience.

A farmer stands by a window with his perfect tomatoes and shows them
to my mother. In his palm he slices one open for her, and sprinkles it
with salt. The salt draws the juice out.
      It is many towns and a long night for us. My father's imagination hybridizes
                        into monster crops.

MISSING

When it happened I camped out all night hoping to hear a leg drag from page to page, then I went in with all my gear and could barely breathe. I made it to love (n.), dug holes and inserted tubes, propped myself in a chair and promptly fell asleep. I dreamt of air going in and bubbles ascending from its depths. Finally, I closed its cover, attached wheels to it and pushed it from place to place. It has been like this ever since. Where she is, I'm not sure, but a lady she is not, among the fingers and gloves and slippers. A ghost of her perhaps in the servant and in the cloth. Some of it Greek, most of it lost. Plenary in volume, black ticking and muslin. At times I wear an entry and catch her scent. At the airport, I run my finger down the words as if they were plumbers. What I need is a nanny to keep my child from crying. What I need is to stick to the task. She tripped and fell, my own mother, into the dictionary, precisely the week my tissue and blood wrote its own codex. It's amazing that with so many words at her disposal she hasn't sent me one. Why not make use of the key to utter a thing: myth machine anger. bull brute cry. bon as this azure. What are the sounds for but to hear what isn't there. An act of sliding, a waterproof coat, a spatula, a wedge to be driven. It's a given she's still living. You can tell by the trails she's left across definitions. And with these fasteners and these rails, one can tame the thought it was an abduction, not a fall.

DEAR STRANGER,

Our plane that night cut through sheets of ice, cleanly and then through clouds. Close to the ground, the sheets turned thicker, the plane's engine started to cough, we sat there each edged in by the fear of death, and also the armrest. How does one survive one's desire for another, I asked you, to ease the tension. How does one survive these flights? The ice turned to sheets of paper and as the plane ripped through them, they doubled in size. We read each moving sheet, which contained questionable instruction, I was not helpful and said they were poems. How does one survive one's desire for big answers, and you grasped my hand as if I might leave. O, the mercy of the body, trying to out-run history. When finally we landed, our plane bullied its way through police cars, pedestrians, SUVs. And ahead of us, another plane curled into pieces. Here was our future, we shall rise as cones of smoke, our casings shall feather weightlessly to the ground. But you reasoned, "That's not us, they must've had a drop in pressure." We made it out and over monkey bars and into a playground, where we sat and waited. The papers were stuck to the plane, everything not said, my waste and the waste of others. And more words irretrievable in the overhead, as in the heart. Sometimes I imagine dropping into the ocean with my inflatable seat. The mercy of the body able to float, until it tires and gives in. It's funny that the best part is no longer having to swim.

THIS IS A FILM ABOUT A STITCH IN THE SKY

The above image shows two pages from a book on silent film.[1] In the film[2] this still comes from, the woman might be seen as gesturing toward the tree or simply walking forward with her hands outstretched. However, its reproduction in book form changes the potential relationship between the visual elements. The seam between pages can be perceived as part of the image instead of obscuring it. The thread can be read.

What might a stitch have to do with these people? Instead of sticking to the world of the film by mentally erasing the interruption, I prefer to project another, parallel film, a sibling film where a woman finds a thread pulled through the air in front of her. She wants to touch it. Part of the thread is apparent but part of it is sutured into a space that can only be imagined. What does the back of this particular sky look like?

This newly spliced film would contain residues of the old film. The man with the rifle leading the prisoner in the middle doesn't disappear. Instead of filling in the part of the tree that falls off the page and touches the ground, I think about the tree as hovering in the air and having a flat top and flat right side. This way of seeing mixes the organic and the constructed: the natural outgrowth of tree limbs and the rectilinear qualities of the page. By treating the habitually invisible or accidental elements as aspects of the narrative, an opening is created for a new, flickering set of perceptions.

Feeling the picture shift like this makes me pay attention both to what I'm looking at in pictorial space and to what I'm seeing as physical material. In my poems, I want to point to the stitch at the same time I keep the people in focus. I want the space of the poem to circulate between the stitch, the people, the tree, and the squeak of the glossed page when my thumb and forefinger touch it.

[1] Liam O'Leary, *The Silent Cinema* (Studio Vista Ltd., 1965)

[2] *By the Law*, directed by Lev Kuleshov (1926)

DEAR BIRDS, I'M RUNNING OUT OF NUMBERS.

Whenever I look at the clock it's always turning 1:23 or 5:55. My mouth is always a three or a one. Everything I see wants to be shaped like your wings when you said *I last saw her out in the rain*. She said she got lost for several pages, thinking glass was the x for my outstretched arms. Incidentally, she was unimpressed by the house of cards you constructed out of litmus paper. We are all so far from home. I remember the way she'd hold a parasol against the sun, watching carp lunge onto rocks, like being able to walk made us the solution for water. I don't know how many times I've called a stranger sister.

DEAREST SISTER, SUGAR IS SUFFERING SOMEWHERE IN WATER.

When I'm talking to myself in the rain I'm speaking to your frequency. Today your voice was on the radio saying *Wolfgang Amadeus Mozart died of rheumatic fever* like it was the last digit of Pi. What do you want me to do with that? I'm thinking through a skin of wet cloth. I'm an exponent of everything you've ever said. I can feel your wavelengths growing in every bite of apple, every damp step of ash.

THE SLEEPER DEVELOPS IN THE CHORDS OF MY THROAT.

To collapse our necks with glass. To pronounce the latent hive in her chest.

Look we are a loom and a fissure straying.

The voice you hear means blind or ghost. Threads.

If I tunnel or extract to pronounce our blanks.

Your medicine is a negative mouth. A still between frames. Skipping.

She uses her radio voice to assess the tension in a phonograph.

To collapse her frames with utterance. To assess the embedded throat.

I am a chord and husk of that gloss.

She develops straying retina and all her tones stammer.

We are threaded in thirds. Film slivers. Transistor medicine.

I am the retina and throat of that ghost. Recorded in her blanks.

She enters through the fissures. The vagrant space between our eyes.

To pronounce the blank in her mouth.

We develop in the space between revolving and breath.

Gloss in the chords. Detached.

I am a hive and shard of that voice.

If she speaks slowly to collapse her veins with smoke.

I see nothing but shimmers. A negative mouth. Skipping frames.

Between a tunnel of blank and running. She extracts my projector voice.

To say that ghost stammers. That gloss stings. Transistor.

INSIDE ANY GOOD SONG SOMEONE IS LOST

There is a splash. There is another splash. There is another. There is a man a man two women a boy and a boy. Something else. Someone else. I can't see past the wheat and birds I can't see. There is a singer. Is there a second singer? There is. That is, you can record yourself from the center of a parade. The clouds are large. You are little and the clouds are so large.

THEY SHOWED A FILM OF ME WALKING TO WATER

A woman walking beside me. She hears bees when she swims was the title. The scene folds out from the flat stone the sun is.

I am watching her trace the air where I was but they want me to see something else, her water double, a paper palace, but I am on a bus again.

She was folding her arms to make a mirage, touching the snow in a sentence. She knows I know I will disappear tonight, a time-lapsed splash in my place.

Inside any good song is a small piece of snow is the one I am listening for.

No more poetics.

from NOTES FROM IRRELEVANCE

One may be so
dispossessed as to
emit the frailest of leers
at these mood lit
passers-by. Who shall
commit their organs to
a solution of gold liqueur
and pigeon shit dispersed
as conditioned air with
a feeling for no inside
world, no groping of hands
within the ribcage? This
shortcut through projects
for the aged almost
tames a barely rendered
playground into an
illusion of use for those
pesky pigeon-feeding
bike-riding dogs! I will
not grovel ethically before
just what is. I will never
abandon my desire to
recede into and out of
interconnection just
because I can't help
spreading out in strange
places from some need
to be seen in my life in
the world alone. Diaper
fornication just wants
to be pure, to pay down
the card's balance, to

handle degradation with
style, to lie as safeguard
against complacency,
to wear the interviewee's
headphones between
innings, to slouch and
deliver until fading into
completion, to merge with
the enemy and absorb
its best qualities, to puke
in the corner and ask
for wipes, to love the evil
kitty and its scratchy
glass eyes, to give in at
every moment and keep
it perfectly quiet. Getting
some absolution out of
the way comes first,
followed by feeling like
a relic, then instant
blistering of self for
indulging self-pity
before another kind
of desire tickles the
psyche. That's one
moment. The next
slightly longer moment
consigns an empty hallway
to emblem of future.
Were one detached
enough to dismiss
operating from anxiety
in order to be a ruthless
collector of materials it

might work to combine
radical progress with
institutional acquiescence
in the name of movement.
Reading the Times by
neon green light in this,
my neighborhood of
delusive transisting,
cleaned up for double
decker tour buses and
their radio-voiced waves
designed to make a
museum out of the dug
streets. I love the view
up first ave on a clear
day, a straight line north,
a wiped out horizon
stood on its side to
appear climbable above
the ordinary hum of
death that is traffic. I'm
for Nero's spinning
party room and against
unmanned drones,
though I like the idea
of a manned drone,
which sounds like every
allegory for society I've
ever paid money to
view, yet the rundown
parallel jism tracers are
One in the thick of
authentic greenery no
longer natural. I cancelled

all sense of class for an
afternoon just to impress
your penchant for casual
proto-symbolic gestures
of deep irresponsibility
that secretly (not so)
afflict routine with
love's wilier feints.
Forgive me. It was time
to make a break for it
and honor a decade's
worth of complicated
walks. Cosmic interconnection
of all beings?
Check. Futility of pain
management as source
of humor in outlook?
Check. Controllable
vices for purposes
of a secondary level
of interior life, an echo
of conscience trailing
out? Check. A sense of
time as discontinuous
in its spread while simultaneously
expanding
on a surface line that
is only a reflection
of a sense of a line?
Check. Total distrust
of command but for the
contradictory moments
of necessity? Half-check.
Digging the ecstasy

of swinging? Yes. Laughing
at the tree? Is the tree
funny? Yes. So what if
the rain is friendlier
than your ever-slithering
definition of work, or
the chip in your pocket
is merely a lifeline for
complaint superseding
the hardy constant tributes
life makes to acceleration
of everything but generosity
freed from the promise
of entering history as
readable image?

My tendency when I write shorter poems is just to begin, with not much more than a hint of an anticipated structure. I don't know what it is, but I want to get right to it—I tend to lose the impulse if I don't begin right away. I'm more interested in choosing my vocabulary as unconsciously as possible, trusting my instincts for whatever words might follow, and seeing what comes of it. Whatever words might be hovering in my environment may fall in. Of the poems in this anthology, one is an allegory written on the subway while commuting to work, one is a surrealist extension of a line by Marina Tsvetaeva, another a conversation with Robinson Jeffers. The other two suit their own occasions, familial and otherwise. The purpose of these poems when I get this particular impulse is for them to be works, inclusive of their surroundings and reflecting for me what I might be thinking about, and hopefully beyond that. Cut-up, erasure, quotation, listing, collage are internalized to an extent, and words do what they do to the person. I try not to take my relationship (or the audience's) relationship to any particular word for granted. A good poem keeps opening itself up. Collision and fragmentation are essential to the sense of representation, as is honesty and directness when that is what is required to say. I am also always writing out of a need to keep writing. It is an extremely grounding part of my life, and I process a lot through it.

LITTLE PIECES CONTINUE AS PIECES

A man says I am this, standing on it
a woman says this is unforgiveable
this will be destructed or not
a style of moment we have
sometimes we share this
I talk to the taxi driver offer
some directions "I can believe
50% of what you say" he says
and laughs we are both named buddy
great cabbies mutter in foreign
languages and sing to themselves
I keep thinking I am 2 years older
than I am getting farther from
my youth but I am also just in
one extended moment I hope
when I close my eyes you are
still there and so am I
I find you on a street corner
another one is chasing his kid
in that playground the gray kitty
rests nearby how is your extended
moment I asked but now we are
just words going over a bridge
whose shadows make us more
and less clear this grammar is
not something I will pretend to
control or master I have no
project but contention
and the monument is already
there as we fade into it

SOME ANCESTOR OF MINE
after Marina Tsvetaeva

Some ancestor of mine
      probably spilled ashes all over himself
clumsy sot, while protracting a curve
      against the abysmal specter of infinite life.
This ancestor of mine kept a flock
      of pigeons tucked between his legs.
While the sky wept acid he slept under the bride
      waiting for the day she would stand up inside him.
If he could only weep he thought, but he wept every day.
      He was a fuse; he wept locusts in a jar.
Cherry trees grew out of his collared boasts.
      That he was doubled was inevitable, but if
ever there was a bucket to the well some oaf
      would draw from its over agitation,
looking to spill blood from the air.
      That ancestor of mine spoke through a prism,
but couldn't tell his speech from the ankles it shattered.
      Failure was the only vindication for his kind of comfort,
starving its puppets with rain water.

MOM AND DAD IN A PHOTO

a tiny blue metal race car grandma
gave to me when I was 32. There's
an obelisk now in Skeleton Canyon.
Maybe you're too close to the speaker.
Tell the Arthur Lee of Love confrontation
story. The tender does not approve of our
vulgarity. Double vocal for airports,
weekend and holidays. Numb grids
that represent human inaction. An incidental
arrival? Why that landing? The speaker of
the poem seems baffled to be in his/her
time continuum. Blind Willie McTell, Blind
Willie Johnson, playing together on the street corner.
Turn down the harp and make it feel more
distant. The next few minutes could hardly
be identified as words. A few firemen later,
the benefit of a lifelong love was clear. A locus
Of abnormal sensation. Harder to keep an
indiscriminate man from slaughter. Off state
extemporaneous crushed weight. Consulting
the at-bats for ideas of speed. I will be home
when my shirt is too dirty to wear.

DISTURNINGLY

I am feeling feeling the pathogens working
whoso reconnoiter with the toes and socks
at a later spill, damn,

when I am reinvented I wish to be
a fizz or a trinket, the kind they sell
in every supermarket in Hell

Hell is a silvery relish
it's a place where people
breathe backwards and
writhe sonnets on tasers

fear this, you'll get good
at it after a while

so shineth the dingbats
and the cunning teeth
of the zaph chancery.

shine they
who shineth sway
I always say.

FOR ROBINSON JEFFERS

A myth becomes a public dream
will be stains of rust on mounds of plaster
Being used to dealing with edgeless dreams
I fell inexactly six down the stairs

My foot's bummed into doom
builds its monument mockingly
they will say we have none in common
the honey of peace in old poems

Salt smog smoke and walks politic
have disfeatured heroes for great lines
belaired in the rock
Unsheathed from reality like Hart Crane

SUSAN BRIANTE

RUINS, CAMERA, FLIGHT PATH

While I wrote many of the poems that would become *Utopia Minus*, I was also writing a dissertation on ruins in the American imagination. My "ruinology" focused on contemporary teardowns—the housing projects, strip malls, and half-built office buildings (Robert Smithson calls them "ruins in the reverse") that make up much of our contemporary North American landscape. We tend to associate romantic ruins with a revaluation of the past, but contemporary ruins remain "unseen," speaking to social and economic histories that we often want to forget. My work became as invested in tracking what was there, as it was in uncovering what had been erased.

The Iraq invasion and occupation began on March 20, 2003, and "ended" officially 8 years, 8 months, 3 weeks, and 4 days later. And during those years—while additional conflicts flared and blossomed, while I read about ruins and wrote poems—I was struck by how our domestic landscape remained strangely unscarred. My parents tell stories of lights blackened along the New Jersey Shore during World War II. But over the course of the Iraq invasion and occupation, it seemed remarkably easy for many of us—especially those of us from certain socio-economic classes—to move through our lives witnessing very few external signs that we were waging war at all. Some of the poems in *Utopia Minus* seek to chart that absence as well.*

In "The Book of the Dead," Muriel Rukeyser famously explained: "Poetry can extend the document." And in the opening stanzas of that poem as she described a photographer unpacking a camera, she also reminded readers that poetry can *be* the document. Over the course of that remarkable work, Rukeyser not only chronicles the Gauley Bridge Mining disaster but she contextualizes the event against national legacies of injustice and oppression. By the end, she asks her readers to "widen lens and see... new signals, processes."

It is the work of a lifetime.

I write this just a few weeks after moving to a rental house under the flight path of the Davis-Monthan Air Force base. I am learning to breakfast and read to my child and write my poems and fall asleep to the growl and rumble of jets. I am looking for a new metrics and new ways to use the lyric to gauge those "signals, processes" that shape our lives and mark our complicities. I follow the stock market. I watch interest rates. Sometimes I check the headlines on my phone to make sure we are

29

not at war, and then I remember we are already at war. And I am grateful for the sound of those planes—because they don't let me forget.

---

*Are these "political poems"? How could they not be? If you can tell me how to disentangle my life (by which I mean how I feed myself, support my family, drive myself to the poetry library at my new university) from the web of privilege and oppression assured by my first-world birth—then I will write poems without politics. Until then, we remain implicated as does our poetry.

NAIL GUNS IN THE MORNING

Nail guns in the morning from the street behind my house,
Outside: tin roof, cement tabletops, "vast maw of modernity" (Sontag),
the UPS man, someone has painted all of my windows shut.

The study of trauma comes shortly after the steam engine,
an affliction known as "railway spine," characterized by headaches, fatigue,
difficulty in breathing, reduction of sexual potency, stammering, cold sweats.

Report from Charles Dickens, June 1865, after train wreck:
　　　Wakes up in sudden alarm,
　　　Dreams much.

Storms this afternoon in Dallas
in the parking lot of the Target/Best Buy/Payless Shopping Center,
big chalices of rain, contusioned sky over the east, big yellow bus moving north
toward the dark end of—what?—

this weather, this fiscal year, this end of empire during which I am reading
the circulars stuck in my screen door, ice waiting
in the highest breath of atmosphere.
It will get to us.

I am patient on the living room couch,
let water drain from the kitchen sink.
Last night over dirty dishes, I told Farid
I would never write a poem that just said: Stop the War.

So frequently, I want a witness. Sit with me,
C. Dickens, let me tell you how bad
the food is on Amtrak, how a Pullman position
was a plum job for freedman, how Stevedores once owned the city
hall, how Indians shot at us through the windows of the smoking car.

Stop the war, stop the war, stop the war, stop the war, stop the war.

ALEXANDER LITVINENKO

I found a billiard ball in the dirt next to the driveway
a tear-off, a throw-away, a non-sequitur awaiting me this good-natured morning
beside the neighbor's rusted fence post.
Inside her yard I found room for all of us.
Move the planter to the porch, watch the snow melt from the eaves,
can someone reach the wind-chimes, clear their throat as if beginning
      a ceremony?
      We swallow
unstable atoms in every cup of tea, fields of ice melt at the polar caps.
Find a blanket to lay upon them, a lead-thick thing like those thrown over a lap
by an X-ray technician, before he slips from the room, flips a switch,
a circuit completed/broken   bones   as white as a silence
as when   returning from work,
      we reach the top of the stairs, call out: "Is anyone home?" Every day

another source of heat expires, bones from another
century. Winter
bends toward porchflowers, stills the windchimes, kills the vine growing
through the chain-link.

If you swallow the right pill
your blood will glow inside of you, if you touch the right dye
it is possible to perceive any corporeal surface, a customs agent
flashing his light beneath our car, checking the contents.
      Where do you want to see?
Imagine watching your own blood switch back its course
round a bend, remake its banks, there
by the river in the darkest soil we might build a city, erect a barbed-wire fence,
      use any means to defend it.

ISABELLA

The problem is that I always want two
things at once: to linger on Egyptian cotton sheets
and to be up at my desk hard drive whirring;
to sit on the dock dangling my feet in Eagle Lake
and simultaneously writing you this letter
about the ripples I send clear to the far bank,
how my toes hang above reeds and tadpoles,
about the family of geese that came on shore
yesterday afternoon and shit everywhere.

I am learning to row. Winds blow from the west.
An oar can act as brake or motor.
The ribs of the boat make a cradle.

Last night's sleep was shallow, and I dreamt
I flung myself over a group of children
with arms spread until my winter jacket
opened to wings. Men torched
parked cars. Police hurled grenades
across a street. And while we huddled
behind a Gap advertisement near a subway
entrance, my father ran towards
the barricades calling
another woman's name.

SPECIMEN BOX

on the wall by the fireplace
we can fill it   with stones, flowers, toenails, pebbles
of shit   or scat   or something else Anglo-Saxon   and indispensable.
No books on Texas   birds, no botany, the rock
is called a batholith, stands 1825 feet,
a large, solid granite dome   where white men
fled captivity, Comanche, Tonkawas, a sword-edged
tongue or a nettle you carry for miles.
          At night the rock moans its way from hot to cold.
Grasses by the highway grow bovine.
What is happening there? a harvest of lime?
In the luminous day by day,   the book was just interruption,
a record of presence, attention. Music
rises from the deep lobes of lung.
          Your turn to tend,
to imagine first a settlement
then something else, to wish to remark   ancestrally
to note in the deepbook a scent of sewage or sulfur,
while wading the tall grass to goats penned in our neighbors' backyard.
Logs from Kentucky, windows from a European farmhouse,
not the machinery I imagine
but the reasons why the water
tastes plastic. Self-reflective, palms open. I never want
to bother anyone with my presence,
          my, my, my, my, my
not even the goats. The fire pitches
its guttural song, wind makes a way through the porchwood,
movement in the musical sense, not transit.
          I rake the fire's hair, the grate
heats, a rib cage, pubic bone.
          A treaty of non-aggression between the Comanche and the first
German settlers here became the only such agreement

in Texas never broken, thus the guttural tongue, the fire
that moves to its end. I am tired
of tending and my thighs grow cold.
"I take SPACE to be the central fact to man born in America,
from Folsom cave to now... Large and without mercy" (Charles Olson).
     On the edge of the creek 2 or 3 yellow flowers out of season,
small earth-mover, tractor, when I asked her to name
the trees—she looked shocked—scrub oak not worth anything.
Does one need to tend to war?   Night catches
first in the thicket above the farmhouse, stones by the creek
moonglow against the field, help me name these constellations:
     cricket, lawn chair, ledger, rake. All day, I watch
the fire from the couch, but should have turned the armchair,
tended the window, dragged a kitchen chair to the porch,
watched the wall-mounted mountain
goat high above the kitchen cabinet, Capricorn,
     eyes to the roof,
your eyes are so much better, so self-fixed, so specimen still.
You lack nothing. I sit close enough
to the window to stir the dogs next door.

Joking in the hallowed space, slapstick in the theorem, the punchline in the hymn, I believe in these things. I believe that humor can say anything, make you feel everything. I believe puns can kill fascists, a well-timed joke can bring back the dead. I believe in power and I believe in its dismantling because I have laughed at both. There is you and there is me and we are building a bridge to each other in language—a good joke builds the bridge faster.

My tendency toward humor, and my love for it, comes from a place of celebration, discovery, and adventure. I aim to think of all things as an adventure. Besides making everything more fun, thinking that way helps me shed any qualitative values I place on what I'm doing now. Those kinds of values make you stop in your tracks and choose a safer path or encourage you to reassess your intuition until it's destroyed. I think laughter has a big place in attempting to live a life that way, with adventure and humor at its center. It's something I strive to do and fail at often.

I hope my poems reflect the way I want to live in the world. I want them to maintain an irreverent reverence at all times, whether that is toward love, beauty, sex, or Being. For me, this is the most honest way I can write, with an askance look toward everything, but with arms ready to embrace it all; so one of my theoretical concerns about all art is that of authenticity, expressive rather than nominal.

There are a couple of roles all writers share that are important to me. For me, writers keep the boundaries of possible experience as wide as they can be. I think about empathy a lot, and how if the human race loses it, the loss compounds, becomes an avalanche of loss: friendship succumbs, then love, then beauty. Other than real life experience, I feel that writing is one of the few places in which we can experience empathy. I am talking of writing in the largest sense, from poetry to screenplays to jokes. I also think it is important to play with, engage, stretch, and destroy language. It is an intellectual endeavor that challenges the heart and mind, and so inspires growth, and growth inspires creativity, and creativity inspires peace.

A silly dance engenders trust, a sarcastic remark breaks the tension. Imagination blooms because rationality slips on a banana peel, and me and you, the ones that get it, look at each other in brother-and sisterhood.

THE WHISTLER

Here I am so selfish I only remember my reaction. Each fact loosening falling away like icicles along the eaves. I once saw one so large & the earth so soft that it pierced the ground below it. I once walked through a spider web so vast, I felt its tug as I pulled through it. I once drove 30 miles at night through pitch-black counties without headlights using only my cellphone light to guide me. I once was so high I wrote a paper backwards and since it was for 20th Century Avant-Garde Lit got an A. You know second winds? I got a fifth wind once during a swim meet. As the fish grows increasingly long, life accumulates like a US Ironworks slagheap. Once my date dropped me off at the front door and I ran through the house out the back into my boyfriend's car waiting in the alley. Once I lost control in the middle of northbound 95 and somehow spun across the median, arriving in the shoulder of the southbound lanes, and just kept driving, direction's pointless. I once bought an $80 cab ride because I couldn't remember where I was—simultaneously building a bed in a refrigerator box stealing gas from the Racetrack flying to Denver to marry a stranger. I once strangled my boyfriend at 65 mph on the freeway until I started laughing so much my grip loosened. Once I wrote the most erotic sex fantasy I could dream got paranoid that someone would read it, chose a password to protect the document, promptly forgot the password and let that define my sex life for years. I once sang *Swing Low* in a cop car and felt like a coward. The only secrets are forgotten ones. I once told a man I didn't want a boyfriend and a week later admitted to him I had gotten married. Who said biography is a story true enough to believe? Who told me they once ate a joint before getting pulled over, but at the last minute the cop car flew past them, worked in a gas station and stole all the money, painted a donkey with zebra stripes, danced on stage with Bootsy Collins, who told me that for one day he was the best whistler on the planet, could whistle any song in the world perfectly, rivaled the skylarks and finches, invented gorgeous sonatas whistling them into the sunset, into the blushing dusk and by morning forgot how to do it?

from FRIEND

Sommer, I'm dying. I get this message on my phone in line at Rite-Aid. Sommer, I'm dying, you scream in my ear at the rock show. Sommer, I'm dying, you write in closing on a postcard from San Francisco. Sommer, I'm dying, it's my heart, Sommer, I'm dying, can you feel this? Is it normal? as we stomp through the snow to get cigarettes. Jesus woke up, but who muscled the boulder away? Some prince kissed the beauty, but who wrote it all down? Let's go to the mummy exhibition, let's read aloud *Fear and Trembling*, let's slow the flow through our carotid. Sommer, I'm dying. Present tense. Subject. Verb. The thinning blood vessel, the soft pulsating stone, retina shriveled and rattling around the skull. I can hear it when I jump. Then don't jump, I say.

EITHER WAY I'M CELEBRATING

They're saying irony is dead.
And for a few minutes I thought

I might die too, a woman
who would buy a fifth of liquor
and a pregnancy test just to see
the look on the clerk's face.

It's always strange to be born
before the cusp of some new age,
hanging onto nothing as if it were

Los Angeles. I remember glaring
through the windshield of the family
Pacer. Watching a thirty-foot man
crack jokes on the screen.

My parents were laughing,
but I didn't get the way something
huge and astonishing could be flat,
could not exist at all.

THE OPPOSITE OF LOVE

Someone is wrong. Light travels slow.
The sun's already dead

for all we know. In Fargo, North Dakota,
my sister and I think we'll die

on a Tilt-a-Whirl. The carnie won't
let us off. Each time we scream past him

he just grins.

Sometimes, it's the world that's inadequate.

I'm worried how many more times I'll tell the story
about peeing in a cop car before someone loves me.

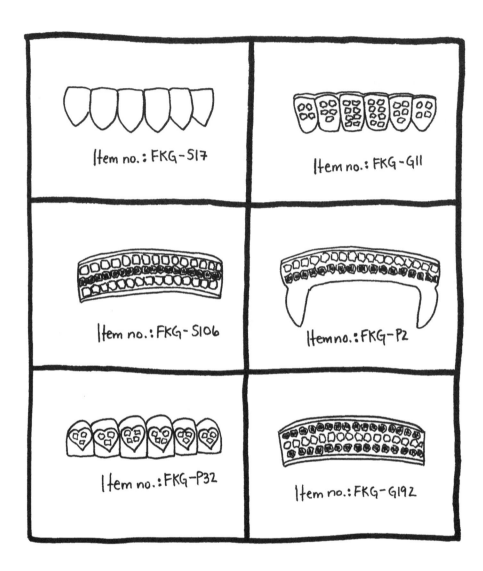

Item no.: FKG-S17

Item no.: FKG-G11

Item no.: FKG-S106

Item no.: FKG-P2

Item no.: FKG-P32

Item no.: FKG-G192

Someone took my book out into the woods and shot it. The book is intimate with violence now in two ways: both as subject matter (violence is what it's about), and as target. The book reaches the gun as its interlocutor. Or, now the book, with a hole right through the middle, needs to be written again.

But when someone shot my book, I felt it got what it deserved, that it had met its precise right audience. No, I felt the book had received its precise right author. The book had been re-authored, or finally authored, by the bullet.

*

In aiming to silence life, the gun makes life more present—that is, it makes available the grief we are already feeling, the grief that one could call the precondition of our living. I don't mean to trivialize or exaggerate. But in trying to understand a nation's passionate attachment to guns, in trying to understand what guns might give us, why some of us want them so badly, I turn to this: only in intimacy with death, in close proximity to grieving, do we find ourselves really living, really alive. *It is the limit that creates the event of life, that is the necessary condition for the experience of life.* This seems to be true, and then it is too true, and the bullet hits its mark and the thing we loved becomes trash.

"I propose to consider a dimension of political life that has to do with our exposure to violence and our complicity in it, with our vulnerability to loss and the task of mourning that follows, and with finding a basis for community in these conditions."

Judith Butler opens her essay, "Violence, Mourning, Politics," with this venture, suggesting that a just community is one that consistently recognizes—and does not banish—vulnerability, fear, grieving—those states that in attempting to deny we only become more and more subject to.

"Loss and vulnerability seem to follow from our being socially constituted bodies, attached to others, at risk of losing those attachments, exposed to others, at risk of violence by virtue of that exposure"—a precise description of social life, I think, though mostly we attempt to locate ourselves outside of loss, refusing exposure. Perhaps what guns promise (to some) is to bring us closer, by way of the metonymic power of the object, to our actually lived vulnerability. If I own a gun, I not only know that I could hurt you, I also acknowledge that you could hurt me. As one senator said to me during a hearing for gun control bills: "I assume everyone I meet is armed." Of course, he who assumes this lives in fear, close to grief. But we need to live this way.

I'd like to say then that the gun and the poem share a common purpose. And that purpose is to allow us these proximities.

Which is why the book is co-authored by the gun.

29.

About human dignity and heavy clouds just above the horizon
but spitting out

flames

About rubber bands and tape

About into the cold and
eddies gunbeautiful

You don't have to make something cry. In summer you'll hear them sobbing into their cells
About—classrooms acquire better locks. About

snipers in black with devices for spying snipers in black are dangerous are dangerous /
About

YOUR MOTHER'S HAIR IS TACKED TO THE WALL

32.

The useless mother's face is green, like a blade
of cut grass sticks

to your
foot

Her voice cold candid flat,
the Atlantic ocean, a credit

card, that

empty

35.

CONSIDER THIS

Consider this: what is violence? the narrowest hinge between lovers and lamps? trashcans and trains? music and muscle? between pillow and plan. weed and wretched. get this, people, there's nothing wrong with a little defense! no reason to be ashamed of sticking up for yourself! stems of leaves slip into the gutter. in and out and in and out and. the light bulb drinks. fire until sunrise. short stem of morning, what *wrong* with him. just walk away. but walk away quickly. consider hot days in the project pool. "lucky" because we had carpet and coke. a woman's breasts are an upside down heart. not at all. we were not at all safe. he wanted to liquefy the self's solidity / within the body of another. because where else? wind, consider it. it's coming from the west. it's carrying a factory smell. we did not know whether, after passing out in the alley, they recovered. // rum in the coke bottles of twelve-year-old boys. what is penitent? what kind? dazzling and tremendous.

"how quickly the sun rise would kill me if I could not now and always send sunrise out of me." this crewless ship stalled in the shoal: what a project. it's an echo-y stairwell. what is well? what wet? the race-riots of childhood. the projects of broken. here's a wander-site: dump-dogs and "boyfriends" with bruises and boils. pimples and penises. light bulbs drink / in corners and causeways. smoking children. dirt-bike riding children. copulating children. children with their pants down. children with their feet bruised. with their hair a mess. eating children. children in school but hiding. in school but running. in school but can't reach. cars with children and houses with children and dumpsters. enough. return:

honey / suckle and candy / bag. and the window drinks. drinks, not impatient, the body is cut. the body is steering. consider the man / fingering his cock slow-driving alongside us. what's *wrong* with him. dump-dogs and boyfriends. asking directions. consider the disdain / of twelve-year-old girls. our huffy walk home. what is violence. nodding out on a borrowed couch. what we didn't get then we do get now. memories tutor / one another. we were not at all safe. consider harm. not what animals do. the fire-assed monkeys, slow-trunked elephants, decorative zebras, meaty lizards. adjective noun, adjective noun, get the pain out of the hand and put it on the page. "Tenderly—be not impatient, / (Strong is your hold, O mortal flesh, / Strong is your hold O love.)" drink not impatient, the body cut. what hand of the man. so wild in the kitchen. not at all. we were not at all safe. moments of / what is a zebra, what is a meerkat? what is a baby, blinking and wrapped? not at all safe. what is my son?

from RAG

The fact is, I never much liked him peonies bloom
It was more or less my goal to ignore or hurt him peonies bloom
Being the proprietor gave me the right to do this peonies bloom
Since it was my property and everyone was my guest blooming
Variously, I disliked his smell, his hair, the shade of his skin in the spring
If the heat goes on all by itself it's not my job to turn it off folds of folds
Once I bent over and invited him to look into my asshole perky stems
Which he gladly did at the top of the stairs five fat flowers
At night I could rarely sleep and this was because of his breathing color of prom
Whatever was my general attitude, for I was full of fun the secret in the stamen
So buried was this fun in my psyche I rarely let it out eat the flower
Spurting like ketchup from a packet I cleared my throat some more spread than others
Had to sometimes sleep under him the tightest one is the one I want
The sensation of my knee against his genitals the most spread open the ugliest
On Sundays I refused to eat a thing color of girl parts
The fading petals a ball of sex unpeeled

from RAG

I had no other alternative
Being on top made for a completely new sense of being white
Now I know the money's coming in
It's a pretty short walk to the philosopher's apartment

I was in love with my father
Especially on the phone
But to ventriloquize the language of the stupefied: I gave it up

I take from my pocket a packet of sugar
How familiar is a fool!
and shame my mouth on a poor girl

And disgrace my mouth on that poor girl's scars
for which I have an enormous pity
I had to do this: I'd missed it too much

We sweat out all the wilderness left in us
Consider the beautiful word "give"
And the harvest moon about to rise

But whiteness is so disappointing
Scrape eyes from the shield, ice from the glass

I can offer you no more
be no better

MY NATALITY IS YOUR FATALITY

I was sangfroid and so I sang Freud and dragged out joints of cliché—say we, may we accept sherry? Manegg was born innately. Let me put an end to son envy and colonialism with natalism—that was my intention, ambition. Nevertheless, I stand up to urinate and wave hello in my halo of amniotic trance. Ugly egg, chicken-sized, and natally late. *At any rate, you have one (or several). It's not so much that it preexists or comes ready-made, although in certain respects it is preexistent.*[1]

GRAMMAR FRAMMAR

Is it not drama? Whether manegg is a count or non-count noun is not parent to me, which is to say, I am in trance, transparent, phonically speaking. Let me put an end to grammar of obedience and colonialism with fetal ontology—that was my intention, eggbition. Event very parent. Correct me if you wish. I am kind of late sing-along. My tongue is forever attached to nipples. Incubate me, terminate me. Frammar, grammar's fetality is a production against trauma.

PAPALESS PAPERLESS

I want to live in a papaless paperless palace, but a small stinky sac will do for now. In my halo, I wave hello to bankers and Wall Street fuckers. Irate, I will narrate.

Definite indefinite, derivatives inderivatives, Fannie inFannie—I stay inarticulate in transaction about the essential articles of English grammar. It is true that the mirror inmirror on the wall is parent to all. Lice eggs duplicate induplicate popping like popcorn, *the superexcellence of American products.* [2] I just got a call that I'll be moved to a hotel.

---

[1] from Gilles Deleuze and Félix Guattari, *A Thousand Plateaus: Capitalism and Schizophrenia*, trans. Brian Massumi (University of Minnesota Press, 1987).

[2] from Antonin Artaud, "To Have Done with the Judgement of God," in *Watchfiends & Rack Screams*, ed. & trans. Clayton Eshleman with Bernard Bador (Exact Change, 1995).

THE MORNING NEWS IS EXCITING

To All Boys and Men!

Dandelions may not be weeds. They are related to chrysanthemums. Girls should. May all weeds dislocate themselves. Girls should. I clench my fist and watch the morning news. Dandelion leaves are bitter yet tender. Girls should. Chrysanthemums are admired. Beware. The early morning news is exciting.

Special Attachment

I take a long shower. Girls should. I have suffered. I have been mistaken. Doctors and nurses know absolutely nothing. I despise them. They know absolutely nothing. I know everything that will happen. I enrage the world. Girls should. My dishes are unbreakable.

Exceptional Attachment

Squeeze plenty. Girls should. Wash and wash then write to the world. The news will break. Just wait and see. I have all the kitchenware. Just bring your clothes. Girls should. I write to the world. My book is taped up in a box. Wash and wash till the smell is gone, blood is gone. I am most bored in the morning.

More on Attachment

Everyone is born wanted or unwanted, but some may be born exceptionally unwanted or wanted. A nation may be wanted or unwanted depending on what the other nation is thinking about. This nation was exceptionally wanted then unwanted because it was thought to be precariously small. Whatever happens to this nation will be revealed gradually even though the morning news is exciting. Fathers, sons, boys are usually exceptionally wanted. At times they can be born exceptionally wanted then unwanted because they are thought to be precariously secondary. This father was precariously secondary. He knew this nation well but he knew the other nation even better. This is what happens when the other nation thinks a lot about a nation and stays an unwelcome stay. There is another nation that thinks about this nation but whatever is to happen will be revealed gradually despite the fact that the morning news is exciting. This father who was secondary amongst wanted existence had sadness about unwanted existence. Nevertheless this father took pictures of this nation before, during, and after the war.

A Blue Suitcase

Twin twin twin zone. Cameraman, run to my twin twin zone. A girl's exile excels beyond excess. Essence excels exile. Something happens to the wanted girl. Nothing happens to the unwanted girl. The morning news is exciting. Excessive exile exceeds analysis. Psychosis my psychosis. Psychosis her psychosis. Pill her and pill her and file her and exile her and pill her and pill her till axis and boxes and sexes.

Let's Get Loud

STUDENT REVOLUTION = APRIL 19, 1960, SOUTH KOREA

S = SEX = FILE = EASY

R = REPEAT = PETITE

A = ASS = ASK

19 = CENTRAL = COCK = MAN

1960 = WANTED = SOMETHING

S = SOUTH = WORLD

K = KOREA = WORLD = DEAR NATION

It is easy to tell the uniformed students are following and something is blazing. On the other hand the morning news is exciting. Of course near narration is exciting. Cameraman, run with the shoeshine boys and watch them die. They made themselves into a single mass by locking their arms and shoulders and moving like a tide. Hence bring down the world. Whereas the elite was petite the center was cocky and manly. As you can see dear nation was petite and wanted. Hence dear narration. Watch me shine.

Nothing Happens

I have written LETTERS. I sat in my car and cried for a long time. Then I lashed out. I decided to write a long letter. When nothing happens I cannot repress my rage. Far nation calls you and you go. You run with a camera. Far nation pays you to run. Hence morning news is exciting. Far nation pays the petite nation to run. Naturally you run and follow the bomber. You sit behind the electronic warfare officer and puke. Manage your fear, far narration is here. Everyday life seen through everyday eyes. Troops on foot. Flashes of napalm intercut with everyday man singing and playing a guitar. Flashback to Ho. Everyday woman and infant looking distressed. Everyday man's guitar. POV from F-4. Very low level. Series of aerials looking back over everyday craters. Glistening water.

Aerial nation for everyday eyes. Hence I wait for the morning news. She has written that nothing happens to the unwanted girl. What error.

She's an errorist.

from DIARY OF RETURN

August 8, 2002

I arrived below the 38th parallel. Everyone and every place I know are below the waist of a nation. Before I arrived, empire arrived, that is to say empire is great. I follow its geography. From a distance the waist below looks like any other small rural village of winding alleys and traditional tile-roofed houses surrounded by rice paddies, vegetable fields, and mountains. It reminded me of home, that is to say this is my home.

Close up: clubs, restaurants, souvenir and clothing stores with signs in English, that is to say English has arrived before me and was here even before I had left. PAPA SAN, LOVE SHOP, POP'S, GOLDEN TAILOR, PAWN. I followed the signs and they led to one of the gates to Camp Stanley, a heliport, that is to say *language is not be to believed but to be obeyed, and to compel obedience.* A woman in her seventies lived next to LOVE SHOP. She was taking an afternoon nap. She has never left below the waist and eventually came to be regarded as a great patriot by her government, that is to say she followed the signs and suffered from lice infestation during the war and passed the lice on to the GIs. I followed the houses that reminded me of home. They led me to another metal gate and barbed wire. Another woman was having lunch at My Sister's Place.

She did not remember which year she had returned except that she remembered hearing about the assassination of our Father, that is to say she was here and I was still elsewhere and *the unity of language is fundamentally political.* She told me a story with her right index finger. Her finger fiercely pointed to her mouth, then between her spread legs, and then her behind. She had no choice under the GI's gun, that is to say she had no choice about absolute choice, that is to say her poverty was without choice and when absolute choice was forced upon her she chose a GI, that is to say she chose empire because empire is greater than our Father, that is to say she followed and left her daughter to its geography and her index finger had no choice but be fierce under absolute choice, that is to say she had arrived home.

October 28, 1992

Yun Kŭm-i's head was smashed with a Coca-Cola bottle. She was found dead, legs spread with the Cola bottle in her vagina and an umbrella up her anus. That is not to say empire does not endorse one planet or Father's umbrella. On the contrary, it enforces *grammaticality* within and without before and after Father sprinkles white disinfectant powder on the index finger. *No one is supposed to be ignorant of grammaticality.*

Italics: Gilles Deleuze and Félix Guattari, *A Thousand Plateaus: Capitalism and Schizophrenia,* trans. Brian Massumi (University of Minnesota Press, 1987).

TWIN FLOWER, MASTER, EMILY

1. Dear Twin Flower,

Only — true men — survive. Prior to military pornography, one never thought about petroleum byproducts. Tarzon bomb — a thing of the past — forgiven and forgotten. Daisy Cutter — lags! Consent is everywhere — Geography — Eternity! Terminate the notion of class when carrying out simulated bombing runs. Division is threadlike — scallop-toothed — a pretense of some kind — willed arbitrarily. It takes approximately twenty minutes to cut the waist of a Third World nation. Excellent yet inferior — this is why — we bang-bang in the woods. It is every man's dearest wish.

Yours, Master

2. Dear Emily,

For poetry — I have you. One need not be a House — One need not be a Nation or a Master for that matter. Delicate and beautiful, common in rich mossy woods, in pairs, we live. We are crimson-pink, particularly in the mountains. The rough terrain is not visible to many, but somewhat green and fatigued, demilitarized! A nod from far away is hollow.

True men — How shall I greet them? Nation building is kind and generous. It is common to decline it. Emily, Shall I — bloom?

Yours, Twin Flower

3. Dear Twin Flower,

Your sister left me — she was cheerful — though maddened — knows the doings of Master. In fact — she lives it! Regretfully small and anxious — frequently far from home —

Do stay! I am so near myself — Your sister is too. Near — Far — how was it arranged? Suicide is not an option — perhaps Resistance. Send me a portrait of your Distance!

For politics — I have Walter — white racism which came to pervade the world was an integral part of capitalist mode of production.

Yours, Emily

4. Dear Master,

I do! Autogeography, I do! Deeply lobed, in defiance of pretentious form, I push a petal from my Gown. An orator, born from jets, never met a translator. Orator, map out a wasteland between the front and the Chinese border. Such is — neocoloniality. I do! Autotranslation, I do! History can confront napalm. Sister's madness is as good as mine. We make the biggest picture in the world. Shallow and spiked, nodding in air, we endure barbed wire. Daisy Cutter can touch us, cut us, demolish our petals. Our gown can stain like a drape. Translator for hire! Hire me. See you at DMZ!

Yours, Twin Flower

"We bang-bang in the woods" was reported by a New York Times reporter in 1950, the first year of the Korean War. A South Korean policeman was about to execute forty civilians who were supposedly communists. The quote is from Bruce Cumings' *Korea's Place in the Sun* (W.W. Norton & Company, 1997).

"One need not be a house," "I push a petal from my Gown," and "Shall I — bloom?" are from Thomas H. Johnson's *Final Harvest: Emily Dickinson* (Little, Brown and Company, 1962).

"White racism which came to pervade the world was an integral part of capitalist mode of production" is from *How Europe Underdeveloped Africa by Walter Rodney* (Howard University Press, 1982).

ARDA COLLINS

I am interested in what the world is made out of. This includes the origins of landscape in the physical world and etymology in the world of language. What are the origins of the names for the elemental components of our surroundings? For star, lake, hill, mollusk, wave, flesh, blossom? How might a sense of origin effect our perception, and what emotions transpire?

Attention to the progression of a word as meaning changes or breaks away into other words is part of how atmosphere in a poem forms. Imagining atmospheres reveals new states of mind through image. I watch a lot of movies because atmosphere is a deep and explicit aspect of form in film: palette, attention to the face, the experience of violence or tenderness, pacing, landscape, the face as a landscape, and of course light—are part of how atmosphere in film transpires. In *Light Keeps Me Company*, which documents the life of Bergman's cinematographer Sven Nykvist, directed by his son Carl-Gustaf Nykvist, Roman Polanski says of Nykvist "You can see the air in his movies." This quality of dimension is a primary feature of atmosphere and in Nykvist's work its intensity is literal. The actor Stellan Skarsgard describes it: "What stopped me in my tracks was the light. It was as though you could grab hold of the lighting, which he had created. It was so enormously sensual, living it's own life. It almost felt as though the lighting was closer to you than the set was—without its getting in the way of the actors in any way at all." In poetry, atmosphere as a presence can supersede rhetoric and familiar syntactic constructions to create a form for speech.

Such an expansive and elusive formal occurrence shows in the vast noun "shale." Its etymology is related to "shell," as in seashells, shellfish, and also the shells of pods and nuts. "Shale" is also related to "scale," as in the scales of fish, of metal, and a scaly disease. By these definitions, "shale" forms associations with textures from the sea with drier, earthier ones, and with the layering of skin. Associating them together produces an image of an ocean that has disappeared through geologic change, or ebbs off as it transforms into a landscape of flora and fauna that emerged from it over time. "Shale," as we know, is also a kind of rock that is layered and pressed. The qualities of the rock overlap with the textures of the other shales and shells. "Shale" is also a verb—the movement of water that makes the sound of the sea. These meanings together evoke the sound of water moving against rocks, shale against shale, and the breaking sound of shells. The formation of fossils through layers of rock and the audible sensation of the ocean occur and form the language in a poem.

153

My longing for you is like clouds

the coming motion

the day's events together.

It's heaven

brick that pale

mandible blue

winter it is

we are in. There is no reflecting

the gold singular upward

mirror building windows

ursine sunset

king metal rose-hue

sunset coming

and coming away.

Walking more than one dusk

to walk into the one still

that arrives

in it a postal ring not yet

reached my ears.

Wail, pale, and sail.

You do shoot yourself in the face,

don't you,

predilected

kiss

I heard your thought through,

catch up.

158

Incandescent, black body
your soul is on the floor. Your earring
by the pillow under sunrise
I want you to come in the window.
An orange in the dark
was like lake air at night
one way to a planet.
The oceans at the gate
rest, sea pebbles
in a pile while it's gray. A meteor
went above the roof
and the tree shadows threw like a lake in the grass.

Wake in bed, and you're out here.

What is it
you think you could
feel this through?

Milk, a wolf, coal, flowers, and landscape paintings
at night in the hallway
and the yard. You're gone forever
but this isn't it.

They smoked ham in hay.
If they didn't sleep through the night
they got up
and worked, fed the animals, talked, lay there,
all of it.

The grass is like licorice
nothing is a replica

did tonight
I meant it
      the most
on the palm horse
      you rose me in it.
Mt. Jupiter
sent back every minute that fails

to the sunset pole vault over a palm frond,
inaudible being, I don't know
the pines in a rainstorm.

112

Life is fucking hard

A pond that turns

darker the world over a forest turned

red. It might show

what this allows. You are so

strangely in my purpose bred.

I sucked on your tongue

while your blood

told me something.

It's a wild accident

I have something

to say, & why

you aren't?

Green without starlight, what's

sore you understand.

I wince and burn

and go

back to what's left

that's upwards towards an hour you can see above

I haven't tried it yet, but

I'm going to see if it works later

I want to hear your

and your voice is the same feeling

I have this idea that

even though that doesn't

I think it's because

I came in the first night and

hasn't since

been throwing

a silent tantrum. I've had no
personal space all summer, it's bats. Last
night I had a dream about moss and wild flowers
that sprang up because spores from the mountains
had gotten into my things. At first
I was wondering, but then they were great.
They were different
kinds of lavender and plinki. Then the fire alarm
went off at five in the morning and
we all had to go outside. It was really jackass.

Whatever remaining radial winter smoke

across a piece of ground. I know this one the best

No one else

what's inside me, my tongue, your tongue

the world

in that heat

All this talk is making me grieve.

It was mild

by your blistering

prose rose woes

See? not a green ray anywhere, not at all like a

sunset, neglect, not a pond, not stars burning, not a white moon burnt

and hidden in shimmers.

Through, I love you and ways, which

must mean

and listen

while it's said

though,

a doorstep; a forelock; pea shoots that glisten

but quickly, yes, and dead.

TOPIC SENTENCES

I write and stranger appears... The third feral feline... Presenting no theory... No such statement exists... Or, literary discourse... Perhaps a poetics question... Its nose to the floor... I didn't come to writing by way of intelligence... A couple days ago a rat died... The poem's person... Silent because of some dirty rag... It wasn't what I had that was allowing me to be... But what was nil, void, prohibitive... A poem is a person-problem... Pre-dating what we've made of it... Centuries over inventing us... Only today began to stink... Scooping up the trap dumped it outside... The poem as a thing of filth... Halting some ceaseless search... Writing is not writing but thinking... Unlike plants eating our pollutions... One cannot see or hear thinking not even in writing... Though we search within it making it not so... Those times I didn't stick up for something, someone, myself... Still, trapped behind this door attracting wilder animals... Thinking must be felt by return thinking... It's out there and endlessly fascinating... Each day a good idea... I'm always thinking of becoming... For people to appear not poems...

THE DOGWOODS

someone will offer to take your body
away from you
at the time it will sound

like a good
idea it will
turn out you
miss having a place to visit

you will have said
yes to this
bad idea because at the time you were
tired and grieving

we say yes
to bad ideas
because they seem like good solutions
to situations we've grown
tired in—
that's made work horses of us

it will feed
the time an answer
but I'm weary now
of answers when
no one has asked a question

once someone takes
this body away you
have to find
ways to meet with it
in the place
it's been taken to
or else it's been taken
twice

we are responsible
for other
people's suggestions—people suggesting
we give them some *thing*

how far one
can actually travel
to see the good idea
forced in greenery

whereas once
you see it outside
the life it's lived
a person you are supposed to
trust but don't know
that well that both
good and bad decisions
get made

changing is giving
myself the body
back

GENE

our parents are all dead
they die or will die
they died you will never
see them again
after you never see them again there is more
time that will pass where you will not
see them again ever even if you die first
you will take the hope of seeing them into the muteness of nature
to die first means that
the length of the branch is doubled upon itself
the wind will beckon to the stranger on the cape
it will not know when you close your eyes
you are facing the self that cannot be identified
you will base your entire life on how
the breeze feels it does not know you exist
you look into black pit and squeeze the sides holding on black pit
you will think you see something
at the surface many times having brought it to
the round opening all you will be staring into is a gaze
the deep well which returns but does not give
we were born to be orphans
if you die last you will hear the will of the earth read aloud by mouthless ants
I think about ants and do not care if they die
you will think about your mother dying and hurry
to create a family to make up for the family you left and who leaves you
the family leaving you is there.

THE GREEN HAS A PULSE

If it throbs it has color
something without color stands up tall
and with too much color smears the belly ripe
after becoming its fuller self
and full of color it has taken on
more than one of itself
the color of its oppression
for those of less color to trade among themselves

while those with some color don't appreciate what's going on
but wanting to keep the little color they have for themselves
in hopes of collecting color someday too
it is only beautiful when taken from its home or restricted within
not becoming the beauty they admire
but outside of itself in order to be seen and desired
to obtain value
or else it can only be appreciated and not owned

beauty has a shady business in which it deals
but others will say beauty is an orphan if not adopted
if we have seen a thing of beauty
we participate in the death or impending death of a life for its value
which becomes one's assassination based on its place of power

this is not to make any of us feel guilty
about loving what is beautiful
we just as soon might be given over colorless
admiring ourselves from afar

THE HERO

Even before having found a pen and some pieces of paper I had already written off life. At one year old I was crawling. My first memory: I stuck a penny into an electrical socket. My mother sprung from her ironing. In a sky blue sweatshirt and matching sweatpants she ran not to me but to the penny melting on my hand. Blue sparks! Life came into focus with a bolt of electricity, hot and external to my systems, overloading me with my limits. I heard nothing during it. Remember nothing of the pain. I realized I could never hurt myself as much as I could cause fear and hurt in others. The first memory is always of trauma. It sears the spirit. When one locks forces with the beyond for no other reason than to say hello, test the room to see how welcoming the reception. Mine was an electric shock—the world recognizing me as a capable machine.

My brother at 4 years old got angry with me. We were behind our house. The back yard sloped dramatically. We were at the bottom of a staircase made of railroad ties. It split in half my mother's two-storied garden, dead-ending in the grass a couple yards from the tennis court. Beyond the tennis court was a thin row of trees and thick brush separating us from the back neighbors whom my parents had called the authorities on more than once, complaining their yard was "unsightly." My sister and I thought it intriguing. Enough loose boards leaning against the house to build a new one. Their house was painted red with white trim, all of it chipping, like looking into a mouth to see rows of decayed teeth, exposed roots and nerves. As usual my brother was playing outside in his tighty-whities. Forgetting what I had said to make him angry, I said it, whatever it was, probably some threat, and my brother in defiance held up a stick long enough to touch the power lines feeding from our house and towards the unsightly neighbor's. I instinctively raised my palms, held them flat and pressed, as if moving the air in his direction. Stop! Even though it was summer my voice turning to ice cracked as it formed. He raised the stick higher, closer to the wires. His armpits were smooth. It reminded me of the soft spot on a newborn's head. Or the back of a pin cushion. He had found some power to arrest my full attention. Afraid lunging at him would motivate him to do it, to strive towards extinction, I could only wait until he'd stand on tip toes and fry his bare flesh from the inside out, his heart stopping right there in our mother's garden.

This happened near our basement patio, sliding glass doors lead inside to my father's refuge where post dinner he'd head with a bowl of salty popcorn. He built his own bar stocked with gin and ice, and next to the counter on the wall hung a plastic head of an old man. Gray scraggly hair and a green corduroy trucker's hat, his skin dark and weathered, and dangling from his throat was a neck tie made from a red bandana that when pulled, water was spit at you from between the gap in his two front teeth while recorded laughter played for 15 seconds. Outside on the patio my sister soaked sticks in mom's decorative cast-iron cauldron until they were soft enough to feed to me, saying THIS IS WHAT WE DO, lying, WE EAT STICKS.

FLAT

Where does the Midwest begin and where does it fall into chasms of ill belonging? Does it include Kansas? What about Minnesota? The questionable states fight harder for inclusion thus embodying the Midwest *more*. Our parents taught us only to be good people. But the failure was that they still taught us to be people until we understood less about ourselves and more about "the species" which doesn't exist, as I am the entire species. As the self diminishes the adult blossoms and I grew into dormant beings.

I relied on hearing—how I was talked to, in what tones, inflections, decibel levels. Silence was the loudest. They didn't have to discriminate aloud in their own home. What my parents were most silent about was what they hated more than anything. They were professionals afterall, and to be professional means to keep one's mouth shut. When my mother looked at one of us a certain way, I plugged my ears. When I see a play I'm not aware of the stage beyond the curtain and therefore am utterly defenseless against theater. Hating the animal for what lurks within the forest it leapt from. But then, the loneliness of it without the forest!

As I mentioned the aesthetics of the Midwest being numb, dulled, tracked, neutered, spade, comprised of little to no information, my eyes went weak like the legs of kids who caught polio and couldn't treat it quick enough. I'd need other appendages to find any sort of strength of happiness. They say the blind learn to rely on their hearing, that other senses excel when compensating for the more important lame one, but instead I think the blind relay the art of the matter of living. If a situation could not be rendered first by sight then it would have to be a translation, and in the translation infinite ambiguities and complexities came forth as the sole murderer who murdered by strangling. You can listen in your own language, but to respond requires a foreign one.

And when translation fell short I relied on the bastard of translation. The mutt hopping around on three legs reminded everyone of the civil war. It began as a reading of people's erroneous responses, an oppressive situation seemingly beyond their control. But mostly it was a lesson in smoking the horror from its hole and describing the basket in the earth that remained. Example by example, the bastard of translation was also a lie, and more horrendously I came to find out, the original insult. Your reflection in a quivering lake and knowing you wouldn't be able to see yourself unless what was there for you to confront was an accumulation of what so easily escapes.

TSERING WANGMO DHOMPA

Jakanjilliweneupahillitophatchapailawattah

I recited my favorite nursery rhyme with gusto for two full years before I realized that *Jakanjilliweneupahillitophatchapailawattah* was supposed to be *Jack and Jill went up the hill to fetch a pail of water.*

I studied English via Hindi and Tibetan. English alluded to unfamiliar concepts and objects that were unnamed for me in Tibetan. It was presented as the language for scholarship, future employment, and independence. It placed Tibetan into jeopardy as an irrelevant language, or a language agile only in retrieving the past. Perhaps strife and the recent national tragedy cast a somber framework upon the Tibetan present to limit its task to, at best, an unpredictable future. The lessons at home attempted to explain history and consequence through philosophy: life is impermanent; life is change; life is suffering.

Not so the life of English with knotty contradictory phrases, nursery rhymes replete with little children tumbling down hills and breaking their bones, and fairy tales. And because the reality of a daffodil, gingerbread house, or a hot-cross bun never unfolded in the way I imagined them to, I began to write about what they might yet be for me. I built a boat named Daffodil that ferried my mother and me beyond the existence of an exile that was chained to hope and waiting. Through such endeavors, I encountered poetry. Poetry received my fear that a thing did not quite fit its own concept. It allowed objects to stray from their being. It brought life to the waiting.

In poetry, uncertainty became something of an asset. It was relevant towards a future while retaining its deep memory. Uncertainty became whimsical, became ambitious, and it became capacious. It also played with the advantages of a memory and looked inward for repetition and return.

I am often asked if I write about "Tibetan things" and if I define myself as a Tibetan poet. The suggestion being, I suppose, that there is something unique and recognizable as Tibetan in my work. Perhaps it is the unfamiliar that makes such conclusions possible. Perhaps the sound of *Jakanjilliweneupahillitophatchapailawattah* reappears in my work. Regardless, it seems premature to speak of the position of "place" in writing, when the process of writing is also a desire to know what that place might be or become. So I articulate self by displacing the notion of an identifiable or static position. Not as a way of negating a presence, but rather to indicate the uncertainty that underlies all I write and rewrite.

MY RICE TASTES LIKE THE LAKE

It is not everyone's desire to swim as a fish.

I have a little dog that behaves like a cat,

it is not his fault he cannot pass the discipline test.

A fault line runs through the city center

sullen as a stretch mark under a dress;

we believe our undoing comes from one source.

An escape plan is our solace. There are words,

there are stories we never tell. She said

on the radio, *My rice tastes like the lake*.

It was a perfect sentence.

EXILE

From a distance, topography is intent

as in, *Where I am from is no more.*

Blood is not a natural conclusion

to kinship despite theories and experiments

where red prefaces emotion. One thought

supplants the other in the sophistry of choice

(therefore, hunger is a project to fit

into the frame.) Grids in the caves

we build attest to an empire

of codes: plaster and cork keep us

afloat. Necessity deigns

the cessation of sound as nails

hold this house upright.

THE CULTURE REVOLUTION

I am wearing a dunce hat.

The brocade's inflexibility

measures proximity to new

crimes. No word for innocence,

no thing innocent; *I forgive you.*

You wear gold. It does not melt

in the sun, but trades

for a lighter punishment.

The heart's flimsy veil

is perforated for a happy

ending. Arms misremember

to hold the body back.

Contrail from a neighbouring airplane draws

a tattoo. Velocity is doing something

that implicates presence. Think carnage.

Carnation. Incarnation. Revolutions

aired on a sunny day. Part of the trick

in being comfortable in a chair

is to sink, and to imagine the ground

is synthetic. Self-help is the best help

but you must read this in a book.

The fortune cookie suggests,

There is no place that is nothing

in the world. The first three words

take all the attention.

The grassland for ordinary people

is the ordinary person's grave.

Vultures find a body

cut into squares. She died of

a stroke. The soldier struck her forehead

with his old boots when his

fist caught a button on her dress.

You must think of reasons

to pick flowers from the botanical

garden. Petrified nerves

is the name of a future.

She watched her mother

jump into the river,

but the detail was not used

in the footnotes. An outline

of a past loaned for a handful

of grapes. Did you just say

my money is no good here?

POETRY'S NEIGHBORLY ENEMY MIND

"A Secret told—," writes Emily Dickinson

> Ceases to be a Secret—then—
> A Secret—kept—
> That—can appal but One—

A later poem reiterates this claim, and may go so far as to assert that secrets aren't even possible:

> "Secrets" is a daily word
> Yet does not exist—
> Muffled—it remits surmise—
> Murmured—it has ceased—

To say a secret—maybe even only to know one—is to forego silence so intensely as to destroy the very concept.

Poetry might be said to be a meeting place for knowledge and speech, a place in which both can come—and more or less keep—together. That said, I also like to think of poetry as a place where the unknown can remain more or less intact, and I think that the best poems both *collect* and *do without* just enough evidence so as to give simultaneous rise to both intelligence and talk. Another of Dickinson's "secret" poems—a short, dashless quatrain from 1873—reads almost like an *ars poetica*:

> The Suburbs of a Secret
> A Strategist should keep,
> Better than on a Dream intrude
> To scrutinize the Sleep.

Maybe a poet is a strategist of secrets, an examiner of an activity who wishes not to alter that activity's odd and inevitable byproducts.

Here's another of Dickinson's later poems:

> His mind of man, a secret makes
> I meet him with a start
> He carries a circumference
> In which I have no part—

Or even if I deem I do
He otherwise may know
Impregnable to inquest
However neighborly—

The mind, claims Dickinson's speaker, makes us strange to ourselves. Akin to the way in which the kept secret in the first poem I quoted is said to "appal" its keeper, the mind in this poem "start[les]" the speaker, who seems have lost her mind in the very act of "meet[ing]" it. Having come upon and considered itself, the mind recoils. To be mindful of the mind is to be struck blind.

But one isn't struck dumb in this blindness; moreover, utterance here doesn't destroy the secretive nature of the mind, but rather renders its secrecy more tolerable. After the flash of the stanza break, the speaker shows us that it's possible to attend to ignorance by way of speech. To "deem" is to declare, and so the speaker admits she can pronounce the mind's circumference as her business, even in light of her earlier claim that she's incapable of making any transactions there. The poem's second stanza presents us with a less-threatened restatement of the speaker's initial obstacle. At this point, the mind is still unable to be grasped by the speaker's investigations, and yet the mind is also "neighborly," which suggests that the mind, having spoken to itself about itself, is now in some way helpful, hospitable, kind.

Just as we might turn to a neighbor in order to borrow what we don't have, we return to a poem in order to recollect both *what* we don't know and *that* we don't know.

In poems, what we don't know won't hurt us.

Chances are, it already has.

FORCING HOUSE

Here's the quick
wish behind

each kicked
door—

manage to hang
from my panic

my love.
Leave

and leave everything
open.

HUFFY

August, the thick end
of summer where I'm
from. I've a grill, shrewd
tools, a bag of glue,
some Neil Young. (The world
eats what it orders.)
My neighbors cough and
wave and wave and frown.
Your youngest cousin
weaves by on a shit-
to-bed ten-speed, two
crutches tucked under
her too-white right arm.
This is to refer
to almost falling
from falling. It's a
dream I'm not ashamed.

IOWA CITY

Compelled to pretend, I get
all elderly. As in *beer was a quarter*

and everyone would dance.

That boy is cutting buttons from
his jacket, sad miracle — that girl,

that one there, is collapsing a bird.

Graveyard. Graveyard.
Graveyard. Groceries.

I'm the only one on this bus.

COUNTRY AND WESTERN

The stars

here are hammering
the long-abandoned dancehall,

its floor adrift with ceiling, glass,

appliances, and leaves.
Take me apart

into my animal, darling.

I am not safe
to take apart.

I will sleep with you to breathe.

TO THE WRITER

Another cloud spun to nothing, one
of nature's more manageable kills.
Another borderline-meaningless morning save
for everything. You claim you kissed
a certain picture with such patience
you became it. So who hasn't?
You're of one long weary trouble;
you wear your hard mind on your hand.

Thus, your dumb touch, your clunky
fuss, your little millions. Your stomach
newly stuff with amputations. Quiet
and furious dots of distant rooms—rooms,
I would add, through which you'll never move
or sleep—begin to mean. In one of them,
humor, collapsed in a painful curl, an odd
head at the back of its throat. It's what's to bleed about.

C.S. GISCOMBE

ON *PRAIRIE STYLE*: HABITATION AND POETRY

For me, habitation has, within it, a whole slew of unsaids and relations. There's the cultural value of owning your own home (that familiar phrase); and then there's your house's "real" value, the ever-changing market value—websites'll tell you what your place is worth in U.S. dollars. What can I get for it? Well, that depends (as the real-estate truism goes) on location, location, location. It depends on the neighborhood, on the place's proximities and juxtapositions, on its relationship to other human settlement. When you market your house or your apartment you're also marketing that other human settlement—who are you going to see on the street as you disembark from your new address? At this moment—the moment of this question—the issue of marketability places the human and the habitation on the same level.

And—this in response to your concern with "poetic practice"—I'm thinking of poetry as a gift economy; that is, I'm thinking of the worthlessness (conventionally speaking) of poetry as property. This is, I think, a profound strength that poetry has, its off-the-grid existence…

Where do we live? And who is this "we"? What's the range of assumption behind the question? Who's included? Who's excluded? Increasingly I'm finding myself interested in range, in how variation takes place over a geographic space—I'm thinking of populations—human and otherwise—and customs and identifications and, God knows, landscape. Much of the "place" of a middle section of this *Prairie Style* book, the Indianapolis poems, comes from the neighborhood in which I stayed in that city—the Near North Side, with its in-progress gentrification efforts, its influx of whites to the streets of Arts and Crafts houses in which black people live now (or were living in 2000 during my sojourn in Indy). The shape of the range fluctuates and neighborhood—one of the big topics in my head when I look back over *Prairie Style*—speaks to this, I think. I hope.

The above is an excerpt from an interview with Mark Nowak on Harriet Blog: http://www.poetryfoundation.org/harriet/2008/08/prairie-style-an-interview-with-cs-giscombe/

NEIGHBORHOOD, PART 2 / POETRY AND BORDER TOWNS

Right now (September 2013) I'm writing the introduction to a group of essays on several topics—the representation of nature on page and screen, music, "the problem of the color-line," monstrosity, the problem of anthologies, improvisation, "vernacular geography," etc. The topics are various but, finally, all the essays are "about" poetry; the book—to be published by Dalkey Archive—is called *Border Towns*.

In the introduction I suggest that, "Perhaps at best is *border town*—the term—the gloss for something that's actually untenable or untenably awkward." No habitation, in the sense that habitation might bring ease. The idea, however, is not that each essay is somehow an example of such a gloss; rather *border towns* is what I'd be tempted to say (or shout, *border towns!*) were I to be asked, *What is poetry?* But I don't wish to say that a poem is *like* a border town; rather I'd suggest that poetry is the range itself *of* places such as border towns (including the approaches to them, by land, air, or water; including their endless traffic; including the miscegenation joke of the border town), that poetry is, perhaps, range itself.

I lean on Ralph Ellison, whose Invisible Man understands his living not in "the jungle of Harlem… but in a border area," to be a joke on the power company; and I lean on Gloria Anzaldua, who wrote,

> The sea cannot be fenced,
> el Mar does not stop at borders.

In the introduction I claim that the best job prose can have is describing poetry.

DOWNSTATE

To have the same sound, to be called by the same name.

Location's what you come to; it's the low point, it usually repeats.

To me, any value is a location to be reckoned with; I would be remiss if I didn't acknowledge how an event could be talked about like it was you or me being talked about.

Or location's the reply, the obvious statement about origin; it goes without saying that pleasure's formidable.

VACANCY

Vacancy is a story unto itself, it homes in when you kiss and are kissed. Indianapolis sits at the horizon—central, hulking, cold as Canaan. I'd be equivocal, I'd focus as much on where we'd meet or pass one another as on the lover's skill. What am I missing? I'd go on and be articulate about the ways love will dog you. Come wind. The city's a house more than it's like an animal.

PRAIRIE STYLE

A sexual image about the prairie ought to be a good idea: it'd have no meaning in a larger context and its existence, furiously local, might make outline itself a high level of vernacular—the image might be the sum of dire and hopeless songs, more of an after-image really. Love might be, in general, a revelation but sex could have a shape or a figure with which one could remember it; the speaker could recognize it or could himself cause recognition to occur. Love might be terror—the hesitation past town—but sex could be content and outline both, until the watcher (or listener) turns away.

Male, female. Black men say trim. An outline's sameness is, finally, a reference. Towns, at a distance, are that—how they appear at first, a dim cluster, and then from five or six miles off; how they look when you're only three miles away. Inbetween sightings in the prairie itself to get across: trek, trace, the trick of landscape. Love suffers its wishfullness—it's an allegorical value and the speaker mime's allegory with descriptions of yearning, like the prairie's a joke on us (among us). Inland's a name, a factory, something to say; the thing upon which the image verges, the thing push articulates.

JUXTAPOSITION

Color will match anything, that's its undoing. There's one thing, then something else comes up. Saying the rhyme extends or carries an idea from place to place. Color's description; say the erotic overtakes you, like color. Sooner or later it repeats.

THE STORY THUS FAR

Image stands in—a hundred eyes, the hump of the present day, wild cards. Night's got a thousand eyes, night could disjoint hesitation, it could equal you. Living appears and re-appears and spreads like what you can't see. Despair *is* selfish, u-g-l-y. It was summer all over Indy—certainly and bare heat everywhere in town, in every exchange. Where's your gift? The big eye, "the compound eye of an insect." I'd rule pleasure, I'd walk behind it.

(for Ammons)

I began the day wanting to read something about the Ravickians to an audience of Ravickian scholars or, at the very least, Ravickian enthusiasts, but I wanted to do this on a day that had the problem where most people hadn't yet heard of the Ravickians, much less their nation-state, Ravicka. I wanted to launch my small country into a world so crowded with countries that many hundreds went about in complete obscurity. Many countries simply had no reputation at all. Yet, they had people, language, and events as much as Switzerland had. And, yet, somehow Switzerland had become famous and these many countries had not. I only wanted my country to be famous on the Internet and to have geography. It did not need to be a member of the U.N.; it did not have to globalize its currency, it did not need others to invest in its debt. But it *did* want to be bordered on three sides and to look east into an enormous body of water. It wanted to be able to say hello to Latvia as it made its way home. I was saying "my country," but I didn't want one of those countries so small that someone actually owned it. Ravicka would not be incorporated. It wanted democracy but also socialization. It wanted governance without a name, something new that eeked out of buildings. Ravicka wanted to be land first, then environments, then people. It wanted to be architecture then people. It wanted trees, architecture, people. Buildings first, then people.

FIVE ENCLOSURES

At night we heard the city creak and move
and stand up and walk around and call
itself in the wind and bring rain and blow
through windows howling, whistling,
laughing. I lay in my bed terrified of the
deafening silence; I was bored, I was too
tired to turn on a light. It was time for
sleeping and being without personality;
you spooned someone if you could, you
grabbed him and penetrated him so he
couldn't hear the night. I didn't know
what the city wanted nor why it behaved
this way, and in the morning could find
no sign, nothing to corroborate what I'd
heard. We marked this time as the onset
of the crisis, those of us who'd heard the
city creaking, while those who slept
through it or were penetrated to sleep,
they, for a long time, didn't know what
we meant by "crisis." It was years before
people began to leave and ironically it
was these who'd never heard the night
that left first. But, I would wake and the
windows of my study would be blown
out; I would toil in the dark room with
plastic and tape and cardboard and nails,
and after hours I'd drag myself back to
bed and sleep as if I'd just returned from
war, though I had not known war and
later learned that war made sleep
impossible. I'd sleep, though, until light
ripped through my eyelids, then would

begin repairing the damage with my right
mind, with stronger hands, and I'd go to
my study and see nothing, maybe just one
pane broken, which I'd then wonder if
I'd broken myself.

———

I wrote a book about a group of friends
surviving a crisis and then the book
became my life. I named it, once I
realized this was happening, once I
saw that I was writing on the previous
day the script of the subsequent day,
in terms of who I saw and what I thought,
as I moved through the city, once
I saw this, I named the book and made
it so that the life I was writing was also
the life I had lived: it wouldn't just go
one way. It wouldn't just be that I was
living what I had written. I had to live in
order to write, and I had to meet my
friends and receive their writing in order
to write, and they needed to see me write
in order to go on writing, and we all
needed to sit in that café and wait out
this crisis that was taking away all the
other writers. And not just the writers but
also the bus drivers and Bello's students
and the people who rode the trains and
the audiences for our readings. I named
the book that had become my life after
the events of my life so that there would
be no distinction. There was no distinction

in my living; there was no break between days. You went to sleep, your body rested, but nothing changed. You woke into the same circling terrain of the city, the same buildings wandering and knocking into each other and knocking houses down, but nothing falling and no plaster coming off, just waddling and knocking and stomping buildings looking all the time normal but being absolutely unconventional in form.

—

I wrote a book where the maps were jumping out of the page, and I couldn't understand them and they seemed to want to escape but wouldn't let go completely. This was going to be my book on Ravicka for the times. The maps were pictures of our living, where we walked, where our monuments stood, where we met for coffee, our bookstores: the grid in blown out detail. The maps were phone numbers that no longer worked, they were addresses that fell off buildings. The maps were the names we called those walking away. Sirin Cucek was a map, because she translated for us. But, the maps wouldn't stay in the book so the book wouldn't close, and this was a problem. Yet, I wanted the maps to represent the city and to do this they needed to be in motion the way all structures in Ravicka were, but this is

not what you asked of maps, so perhaps
I was calling the "conveyance" by the
wrong name. Maps couldn't move and
space couldn't move, yet, within both,
the object world was alive and in a fidget.
The book I was writing couldn't exist
without these maps that separated streets
from sentences, that showed awnings
in paragraphs, that always had a river.

—

Walls created an enclosure in which
dreaming separated itself from sleep and
the body stood up and walked into the
city, but as an enclosed space that was
walking to the wall and drawing a shape
that invoked a figure bending forward
with an arm thrust out, as if in offering,
as if to make room for something facing,
something turned and waiting to be
welcomed, perhaps someone wanting
to descend into the dense, narrow streets
with you. The body draped over to draw
another body, as it ventured from shop
to shop, looking for books and tools and
candles, the hand shading, the hand
making spirals, the body on the wall
reaching back wanting something. I
didn't draw its head. I stopped at the
shoulders; I didn't go below the shins.
I read the wall with my dictionary, the
Book of Gestures by Soudouzi. I drew a
hand that was missing something, then

drew a line from that hand, a thin, fragile
line that came forward, bent, turned,
broke, resumed its progression but now
below the previous line, that moved
toward a letter, that leaned into language,
that reminded me of its body, then my
body, was something like a map or
just a message that said "move" or
just a failure of the third dimension,
when you found out they weren't walls,
when you woke up.
—

Buildings were like night creatures,
looking for an underground, where they
could meet other buildings and make
relations, relations beyond any that could
be imagined by the human mind. They
met in our blindsight, while we turned
our heads to answer a question, while
we were bent in *pareis*. They moved
noiselessly across the city, leaving the
story of their ambulations in our bodies—
how we ached and searched for them.
We never saw a building move but
were always picking ourselves up from
the ground and could rarely find the
place we were looking for on the day
that we were looking for it (it was out
there somewhere). And, though we had
become the story of their wandering, we
had no way to engage them. How did
you find out what was wrong, how did

you say what you needed to say? It had
to be more than description. You talked
about buildings as if they were animals,
but buildings were mostly numbers:
where angles met, the fluid dynamics of
material, how the wind moved them, but
didn't knock them over. The Pouissart
was in cit Barnje instead of ciut centali,
where it was built, because of numbers
desiring other numbers: patterns
breaking, re-threading otherwise.

—

At recess in the sixth grade, I am a celebrity. I tell my classmates stories about myself, articulate the daring and exciting delinquency of my past. With each story, my celebrity grows. Soon, I've told them everything. I have no more stories. I am ignored on the playground, and so begin acting out again. This alienates me even more from my classmates, who come to resent my brutishness, to see it as a virus, which, fearful of infection, they avoid whenever possible. In *The Theater and Its Double*, Artaud begins with a lengthy analogy between the plague as a psychic entity whose contagion might be a matter of will and the theater as a sort of disease that carries a potential simultaneously destructive and redemptive. Because of my classmates' preference for stories over the participation, even the passive, observational participation, required of witness—the theater of actual events, my celebrity was willfully deflated, cast aside, allowed to curdle into something dangerous, something unapproachable. Something adult. This something was itself a kind of theater, the kind which, as Artaud notes, "causes the mask to fall, reveals the lie, the slackness, baseness, and hypocrisy of our world." If, as Joan Didion famously wrote, "[w]e tell ourselves stories in order to live," then what happens when we've told them all, when we run out of these stories, when we have to live in order to tell them? This is the point where the chatter and babble of the adult world suddenly becomes intelligible. This is where the poem begins. When I was about twenty, I remember sitting in my room one night, annoyed with something my housemates were up to, and a bit bored with whatever my other friends were doing. It was one of those evening where you just feel aimless, off-balance, agitated. There was something gnawing at me, but I didn't know what. Then, out of nowhere, a procession of sirens passed by my house. I mean there were fire trucks, police cars, a few ambulances, lots and lots of noise—sudden, alarming noise; then, nothing. It was dead silent for maybe a second or two before the sirens picked up again. This time they seemed to come from every direction, as though they were surrounding the house. But the pitch was off, all wobbly, a weird vibrato, like electronics trying to run on nearly dead batteries. The sound wasn't coming from the sirens at all. It was an animal sound. It was every dog in the neighborhood at once attempting to imitate the noise. None of them could do it quite right, but damn were they going for it. It felt simultaneously sad and triumphant. It was the exact moment I decided to be a writer. I'm not writing the noise of the sirens, nor am I'm writing the noise of the dogs. I hope my poems take root in the silence after the two have sounded: mimetic chatter and babble moving paradoxically from intellection to imagination.

TEN WAYS TO PUT TOGETHER AN AIRPLANE

1.

Turn toward the undifferentiated vastness in the first of all flowers.

2.

Turn partly in delight & partly inspired by the sick awe of rebirth.

3.

Turn a weakness of the libido into the asset of a well-stocked garage.

4.

Shatter utopian tendencies against the earthly ballast that anchors them.

5.

Turn a spiritual aspiration into the ill-omened echo of a dog's far-off cry.

6.

Turn all animals into theologians, psychotherapists, classicists, & art critics.

7.

This theory would liken flight to a kind of castration of the intellect.

8.

Engage in nothing on the fringe of everyday activities save that of forgetfulness.

9.

Turn the sonnet like a saw blade upon the woodsy fixity of received form.

10.

Launch into the air an asexual organ of reproduction. Say it: fuel equals fear.

TEN WAYS TO TAKE AN AIRPLANE APART

1.

A rivet forces proximity on two sheets of aluminum. Violence to the hawk and violence to the horse, together, build a third kind of animal. Wholly subdued, hanger-like. This tangential harmony—impossible as a mountain in the ant's understanding of an airfield. Nothing's joined that wasn't broken from itself; thus, the sexual elevator crushes a man holding a bouquet of lilies. An orchid lashed to a tree proves original theory untenable. Is this how you underline your way into the pantheon? Pegasus was a horse. The airplane, an automobile. A pillow for earth-bound egos purified in upper air. Orgasm tears the plane apart.

2.

Was it a flock of black helicopters I mistook for an early turn of evening? Interrogation's a landing pad in a garden. A tiny X hovering over the question: what variable doesn't love wilting? The only thing that pulls a fly from the air is exhaustion. Grounded by a noisy ionosphere, cut in half by a cloud, adrift in the always concussive intermingling of imagined things, my desire remains the same: explode the word "construct."

3.

I give you the undisturbed image of the airplane, then a sun tied to the sky by schematics like a crayon crushed on a blackboard, an interrogative parachute in pastels on dyed paper, implicit as a doorway in the dark or poor Ophelia's waterlogged dress, enough gravelly syllables to lay a runway in every conceivable language, your refusal to land turning away from the rhetorical.

4.

If mutual agreement explains the world, is that ladybug example or arithmetic? Dear apple, the earth, photographed in its entirety, doesn't place you at odds with your animal. That's perspective's job. Nude awareness is nothing new. Who says a cockpit can't be comfortable? Automation never found a gardener in want of work, but seeding the clouds above this mechanical sense of draftsmanship begs the question: is it still impossible to improve upon the ladder? I plant my little doubts and people like little dots can't assemble the airplane from this distance.

5.

A painter hacks apart an explanation of the yellow jacket, the first steps of a descent down the airplane, a relative ladder & yet a ladder, an alloy of zinc & aluminum cast into the shape of relational contingencies, a geometric plane perhaps or perhaps a pipe cleaner twisted into a plane, another miniature trope to model full-scale diminishments of full-scale expansions, an opaque airfoil pantomime, the expansive inauguration of which the inchoately described decomposition of a wing, after all, is the ladder at the end of the airplane or else its attempt to reach an actual cloud.

6. (dissolving aphorisms for a skywriter)
The history of human ingenuity has a somber disregard for the genuinely human.

With every mention of Icarus, the house of buoyant particulars rocks a little on its foundation.

A bird goes to great lengths to construct its nest before knowing there are such things as eggs, but what architect isn't born disregarding?

Building is the most beautiful verb.

It is without language that our bird is perched on a branch of the word tree imagining a grammar flightless.

The airplane's animal image is artificial.

7.

The airplane is a metaphor of annulment, a body whose borders are flayed, districts redrawn to allow their constituents election of infinite stillness for the engine's interior, a platform upon which a butchered animal's organs are to a system for organizing experience as an air traffic controller's contortions are to the weather wedged within a keyhole, which is to say once you open a thing return is impossible. A door closes. A day closes. Eggs plummet to the earth as the ant ignores the orchid and both go on eating their air.

8.

If an annulment of metaphor is negation's landing gear, and contiguity gives the ambulance its atmosphere of maudlin frenzy, what colored siren would smash its medicine against the rocks? Take a few minutes to formulate a response. In the meantime, the question begins its turbulent descent. And afterwards? Afterwards.

9.

The problem of the airplane is falling. Obscure and groundless chronology agitates its origins asserting that the problem of the airplane is falling from a paragraph, from a pair of graphs etched on an apple after it too is bruised by correspondence, forced to stand an aggregate for aviation, subjugated by painting, and slipped into a pocket like an icon condensed into a diacritical mark. So the airplane's century receives its music in microtonal intervals. Flowers break apart. Elevators drift like outlines controlled to an almost infinite degree, a result of improvisation. After its dismemberment, the falling problem of the airplane fails to put a yellow jacket back together. Listen, decibels don't measure sound; they destroy it.

10.

The ideal airplane is paper

Crush it in your palm

slow the sound a thousand-fold

hear a violet opening

AN OLD POEM EMBEDDED IN A FINAL THOUGHT
ON THE AIRPLANE

About fifteen years ago, I wrote a short poem called "Yesterday I Named a Dead Bird Rebecca." The title came to me while in Florida visiting family. Going for a short walk, I passed the carcass of a crow swarming with small flies. There was something so repugnant about this particular dead animal that, although oddly aware of its lack of any sort of odor, I was, nonetheless, overcome by a strong, debilitating nausea, one which I suspect arose simply from the smell I imagined the bird to have. The poem reads:

> were a defused heart
> wintering the clock
>
> time kept
> by counting birds
>
> I'd call flight
> a half-belief in air
>
> a venomous lack
> when the ticking is less so

What could be more obvious than that this poem transposes its propositional way of understanding gravity into the structure of its own identity? Something that lies beyond the purview of its lone sentence speaks to me now as the kind of nostalgia one feels upon watching an airplane pass overhead. It means making distance disappear.

We all have our writing struggles. Here's one of mine: as my children arrived, my mind, my interior spaces underwent serious reconstruction.

I remember hearing after my first-born's birth constant crying—even while my daughter slept. How does one write in the margins of a scream? Did I mention the only being who shocked me more than my infant daughter was my infant son? Did I mention I never quite know who my children are or where they're going, and certainly never at once?

After each birth, previously held writing maxims were torn down and reconstructed on my own terms. I'm startled at the new poetry I'm moving toward and making.

Is today tomorrow? my son once asked.

I need/ed a poetry to admit/embody/advance through internal and external structures its uncertainty. I need/ed a poetry that acknowledges black women exist/mother/parent and write in a multitude of modes and voices.

Being the parent of a thirteen-year-old daughter and ten-year-old son means getting interrupted. A lot. That pattern of interruption and its impermanent cessation at the end of a long day play vital roles in the way my recent poems sound, unfold, and appear on the page. The afro-tongues/songs/ tales my children carry, the afro-tongues/songs/tales I recite, they catch in the crooks of my head.

The aggressive, relentless, investigation, revision, and reconstruction of Writing + Mothering was a complete shock to me. Always tension. Always freedom and control rubbing against one another. It's insanity. It's pleasure. It's headache.

It's a fight to get to the page without a ringing head. It's a fight to get to the page with a ringing head.

So there's no room for bull/y/footprints/prescriptivism.

Who puts their hands on your children? Who puts their hands on your poetry?

It's all unfinished business, really. But I love the struggle in me.

THAT

I grew up with pickles. I slept in
the attic (cigarettes, sheets laced with
smoke). The heat of my father's
brother's old room. Larry Blackmon
painted for effect & Chaka Khan's lips
more like a kiss if a kiss could walk
when it came to life. If a kiss
could have hips & legs & ass—
well, I wanted that.
& if the colors could sweat & strip
me down to my slip, well,
I wanted that, too. Nobody knew
what I was thinking up there.
Though, maybe, they wanted that. That.

POSTING BAIL

Keep missing me, you say. *Armchair, stepstool, tree stump, church pew*, I'm thinking up a list, half listening. Sit back & hold still, I tell you. My list is lacking. Sooner or later, I say, you'll come up on the Sheriff. & by April, the Bondsman on the fourth floor. *Sofa, swivel, chaise.* He'll be waiting for the right answer, some hint of repentance or pencil-skirted decorum, of a straight-backed, arm rested, ghost of a former teacup tipping self. *You'll have to meet,* he'll say with a twist of his belt, *certain conditions.* You'll think of your cousin by marriage then. The one who insisted you "meet certain conditions." The one who wanted so badly to act like a man. *Call this number & that number on this day & that. Then maybe I'll help you,* your cousin by marriage said. Apparently, men make ultimatums. & operate under certain conditions. & look women in the eye & say, *be more professional*, like your cousin in manface. Like the Bondsman. *What's my deadline*, you mutter to no one in particular, changing the subject, leaning back in your chair.

Q.

One of the four Royal Stars is watching over me. Yeah, I'm blessed in these times of nervous weather. The leaves chill in a bundle then scatter like police, off to the next doorstep. They don't step, they don't faze me. These jeans could hold three men. But it's just one of me, girl. Only Son. Only Sound. Only Seer. All this green to gold to red to orange is just theater. I'm the Real. Keep your eyes on the Navigator of Snow and Infinite Gray. I rock these boots all year. What a storm got to do with me? Who knows the number of strolls to heaven? Not that I'm thinking on it. The Heavens know my real name. But you can call me Q. Quicker than Q. But, anyway. Certain things a man keeps to himself. Jesus wept. So I don't. The past is for people who like to play things over and over. Me, I'm on to the next song. Listen to my own Head Symphony, to the Royal Stars. The colors, they thrill me, they fuel these legs.

EVEN DISASTERS

wear white & turn
to honey. A hive

of bad hair days
swarms
inside me. Doom

is lessened out
of the public eye.

The welts, at least
won't show. Dressed
to the nines & too sweet

in the mouth. What
did he mumble?

Something
about insects
garnishing the frosting?

A baby
buried somewhere
inside the cake.

'I WORKED HARD SO MY GIRLS DIDN'T HAVE TO SERVE NOBODY ELSE LIKE I DID EXCEPT GOD'

Candy-colored bulbs frame a girl for a holiday.
If the wicked call from the other side, she doesn't hear. Blinds shut. Devices
blink & twitter. Before it's too late, her mother snaps a picture—anticipates
angst & oddly angled aches, strawberry letters. *Whatevers.*
The mother will mark the photo tomorrow. Sign. Seal. *We're all well*!
—one of the last acceptable print messages. Meanwhile, *Soup
for dinner, again?* What else? It's winter. Herbal constellations swivel in froth. Stir.
She samples with a lean near bowing. Steam on closed eyelids.
Mothers ought to give thanks.
Simeon, she thinks instead, & then: her long-gone grandmother's
tattered Bible, the daughter's overdue library book
concerning States' rights. Why's that? She's hardly felt
hated. X's and O's glow in the daughter's palm. *Look
how easy,* the daughter often says. She is patient with her mother. Blessed
be the child at the center of snow & flu season. She flew past
blessings long ago. So far from a little girl, really.

MATTHEW HENRIKSEN

IN NAIVE AWE

Birth, especially childbirth—no making or creating there. Something passes through us and is born. Men get to participate in this, too, but it's the opposite of hurting. After sperm passes into the egg and those two together pass from the mother into the world, then that beautiful entity already is not the parents' but her own. And yes, others see resemblances to the parents in the child, but parents know most of all that the child is an entirely new entity.

Poems are like that, too, only poets inevitably try to do too much. Poets might try to shit poems out, but the conception of the poem is far more pleasant. That's why men don't understand poetry. Mothers terrify me because they know something I do not. Alice Notley, Fanny Howe, C.D. Wright—all mothers. The pain of and after composition does not relate to the pain of birthing. Poets don't deserve that metaphor.

Are people poems? Certainly, only we pass out of a greater pain that is not our own, while in the poem the pain adheres to the language rather than to our bodies. The *Tao Te Ching* has always amused and amazed me, but while teaching it earlier in the week parts of it struck me as exactly what I am, something akin to a simultaneous peace and confusion not fully synthesized.

> "Who can wait quietly while the mud settles?" Lao Tzu says. "Who can remain still until the moment of action? Observers of the Tao do not seek fulfillment. Not seeking fulfillment, they are not swayed by desire for change."

I want to be that and mostly already am.

From a conversation with Brandon Shimoda

INSOMNIA

I had the busted leg of a plastic chair
to pillow a highway sign's dream.
Once a person on his roof begins to think
about saying fuck you to the particulars,
the only blessing is a stagnant block
in the middle of a dead neighborhood
in a city that has been nowhere since
before you or I were born. And who
and what are we, after words, but
mourners signing a petition at someone's
grave, for better dreams, better meals, better
orgasms, though most of us would rather just
sleep well more often. Jesus, why must it
be so late, so bright and so early?

AFTERLIFE ENDING AS A QUESTION

The world began in wrong. The clouds
prove this by their leniency. As grace

disturbs our sentiment for violence
so the bush lays its ambush of lilacs.

The shortness of the fuse is what
we must suppose God meant
for us to love. Let all songs

shorten the fuse, then
defuse it.

What is love but a negative collaboration?

PARKWAY & BENNETT

The houses darkened quietly
as if the edges had been rained on.

A welt of light remained
behind a hedge

at the corner house
where the mannequin stood.

That was my crazy family you saw.
That was our grass that looked burned.

Those were the screams
of our happiness you mistook.

AN ANGEL UNLEARNS THE LIBEL OF EXHILARATION

I once took the boy to a movie about bicycles.
He fell in love with bicycles.

He fell upon his bicycle, and from. Upon
the thorns, he bled. He learned

his lesson not to learn. The elocution
of the vine evinced the fastened module

of esoteric remonstration. So he blew
his nose and made roses of his cheeks.

So the coward died, who lost his
bicycle. Forever turning, the

desecrating never ends. Amen.

FUCKED UP WORLD

Better present than in any future conceived,
I brought boxes to pack books in.

What can two people make but one bigger loneliness
before falling asleep shoulder to shoulder

in a room of crowded things
the same nameless light hits morning

after merciless morning?
A pile driver in the movie

slams mud until a slum apartment collapses,
Naples in black and white.

Pretend above all to love this thing,
this monstrous idea of a room.

Forget where to put
what and what to give away

or suggest another corner
worse than the one you know.

MY WORK: MY ARCHIVES, YOUR ARCHIVES, OUR ARCHIVES

Language, the great antiquefuturistic archive/hologram of our drives and capacities, constantly needs interrogating as our lifestyles are ever changing, so too must be the grammar of the sounds and tones we assemble to *think about the dreams as they are happening*. And there are the cases when tectonic shifts in our sound grammar, in the way we use language, inaugurate lifestyle changes or alleviate the strain of acclimating to new ways of being in space and time. My poetry seems to anticipate my own most primal and sophisticated yearnings just before they dissipate and dilute into more rational (less intuitive and healing) thought, and to let those yearnings limbo in that "just-before" as discoveries and in that way to carve out a new space, a new molecule between water and will, substance and light, a crevice that makes my own molecular revolutions pleasurable and modal and possible. The grand hope is that what the writing does for me; it does for my readers too, exponentially.

My first book *Negro League Baseball* ventured into the elegiac and came out with a child's will to grasp and let go at the same time, of language, as of human grief; it was cathartic writing, raw and toward a landscape my new work is navigating and making native again. Having been raised in the light of an archive of my father's music (a trove of 1960s Northern Soul LPs with his voice spinning into me from them), it's been natural for me to progress from the elegiac to an unflinching examination of archive and "the creative archive" as a devotional practice, and, especially for Black Americans, as a hybrid space wherein collective improvisation, devotion, and the freedom/discipline binary can coalesce to form and reform a mythos that does not trap every black hero and talent and leader in entertainment industry. *I'm moving forward toward my Myth.*

HARLEM GAZELLE

There's nowhere between the merely savage and the merely sentimental so nowhere snaps into a local

      dissatisfied and free

zone. Choreographing a solo for mulatto dancer about the whites only mourners bench Billie Holiday describes seeing in her childhood church. The dancer is forever/half/ there, haunting each lament with the math in her movements and considered movements. Running toward the bench, then backing away, then leaping toward it again, then scooting away on her ass, as if from some predator, then tiptoeing up to ask permission to join again, then sitting, then crying, then running away, then turning back to ask for forgiveness, then nevermind, then turning back to say nevermind, then being asked to join, then the mourners can't mourn without the math in her movements and considered movements. Then she no longer cares. Then she hides from them. Then she builds a new church, a blacks only mourners bench. That doesn't work either. Impossibility is a destiny and she reaches its needles and spins on them like they mention pop song heroine in gardens from where she's been left out of the myth and written new ones in a two-way language. The roosters catch on and jiggle their coos something urgent and tender as she sidles between them like movie shot in Manhattan stoop feet dawn from now on, dissatisfied and free

ACCEPTANCE SPEECH (MONK'S LOST GRAMMY)

It's really, very, very real to be here tonight in relation to life and death and I'm sure they both love each other

From now on we're only writing love songs or escape songs

Dark, a little dank, smoke-soaked, and blue/ His feet flutter in a soft shuffle, chiming in silence with the urgency of firebells, spinning in slow so binding circles.

We need in every community, a group of angelic troublemakers cause

Everything is happening, all the time

Then he looks away, adamantly, with that shimmering abandonment in every blues man's eye. We are perfectly normal neurotics, crowding around our symptoms with humor and wit, geniuses because of it, helplessly hyper-aware, even when dignity is boring, even when pleasure is more traumatic than anything. Can you dig it? Can you dig it without treating it like dirt? Some of the trouble be angels, be us in the firm poses after dancing, all breath and glances and this is your chance to tempt the good myth to step in your shadow

EXCESSIVE PRESENCE LEAVES NO TRACES

I once read how all the cocaine burst out of Richard Prior like he was a piñata and now the kids from that birthday party, extras in a film of his, all day on a set of burnt grass and hugging balloons, how now they believe in negro angels and try to open every terrible door with a baseball bat and a skull cap or a joke about black habits or a line from a Pam Grier flick like *you don't know love what is*. I read that I was one of those kids. A bulge in the minutes makes us scream inside. I remember now, how we can make sound without being seen. How this scream creates room for silence

THE EXACT SOLIDARITY OF ERAS

They won't exploit me, I promise
The merciless kind of love is truest
You tell your mom
To calm down
To watch some of the movies you watched in college
8 and a half an eighth/where it's more profound as simulation and you can tell the winner
cause they turn him inside out and he remains beautiful, gets even more so. The stunt is
hope. The pipe is hope. The crack in the pipe is hope. When they ask you to play yourself
in the film about your life, there's hope. When you refuse there's a lowdown alley cat
preying on you and you write him out the script just like that. Sometimes it's safer to be
obvious and all you sacrifice is when they ask/I promise. When the drive-in re-opens.
When there's a Sicilian tornado overhead. And it's romantic. Dread is romantic. Maybe
Cicely Tyson was too steadfast. Maybe I'm the one who will get him to quit. You think.
You think Don Cheadle will make a good Miles Davis? You think we know how to play
ourselves yet? Shit, I hope so. I wanna try bye bye blackbird
  backwards

      for a while

and get my habit back

NIGGAS IN RAINCOATS REPRISE

Even alleged militants blame the vanishing of the summer sea ice on *Ghosts* (short version) by Albert Ayler. He disappeared while he was getting his sound together. No one knows what happened but the water high in increments like a crown around his cries and glass is a liquid and you have to forgive your parents for whatever it is and they have to forgive themselves

I would like to use this craft to fly with him

I feel that saddle the morning after and try—again—warm in the habit of our warning and yearning for more of them until

    We finally need to see this reckoning

But when it's time I'm not ready and when I'm ready it's not time—that's fate. And blind in the halo of so-what, so-what, we make it a future

I say, *I don't know who you are.* I say, *It don't matter at this point, I do it all for you anyways* (long run)—Gorgeous photographs of industrial ruins so lush you want to lick them, be them, become a trend. Crushed under the debris, an instrument is so tender it breaks and mends in the same note. Becoming men is like that, degrading, uplifting, denial, lazily caving in Isis and ice until all of our guesses are obsolete we can't see nobody who isn't disappearing

CATHY PARK HONG

SPECULATIVE POETRY

There is no nation but the imagination. Speculative poetry conjures a world that is invisible, a mirage, a false pond. Speculative poetry is the overnight Sims city, a city that is a composite of elsewheres, the city in drag. It imagines the boundless dream metropolis that stitches together factual history and fabulous ethnography. It creates the geopolitical imaginary, building worlds to critique world-building. It makes absurd vatic pronouncements as a means to indirectly apprehend the present. It is the present. The poem speaks in a paper language, a mélange of offshoots, with multiple entryways and exits through its high use of fleeting vernaculars. Its form is code-switching: code-switching between languages, between Englishes, between genres, between races, between bodies. Speculative poetry is inspired by music that beat-boxes, that dubs, that samples. Its enemy is the drone. It has traded in the persona for the avatar. Its emotional range is not mono (not mono-sincere, not mono-ironic) but stereophonic and excessive. If for the Objectivist poet, one must look clearly at the world, what is the thing that is the image when we live in a constant state of "image flow"? Speculative poetry interrogates, lyricizes, and captures the dematerialized thing, our dematerializing world. Speculative poetry does not escape nor does it shape one reality, but captures the song of layered realities.

YEAR OF THE AMATEUR

      Recall the frontier inside us when the business
of memory booms, when broadbands uncoil
      and clouds swell with sticky portals, flavored monsoon,
amassing to a dream of scrambled libraries looping
      scrolls into confessions,
burn your chattel to keep the cloud afloat
so its tears can freeze to snow.
      The voice flatlines in this season of pulp:
The artist makes miniature churches out of drain pulp,
The Indonesian rainforest is pulped,
the last illuminated gold leaves are pulped so we
      gather and watch an otter nom nom
sweet urchin to a pulp.
We laugh softly.

WHO'S WHO

You wake up from a nap.

Your mouth feels like a cheap acrylic sweater.

You blink online and images hopscotch around you.

A telenovela actress hides under your lampshade.

You switch to voice activation.

Good Afternoon! Sings the voice of Gregory Peck.

You look out your window, across the street.

Faded mattresses sag against a chain-link fence.

The mattress seller sits on a crate, clipping his fingernails.

You think of inviting him in.

You do a scan.

Gregory Peck booms: Dwayne Healey, 28, convicted felon of petty larceny.

You don't know what to do so you pet your ceramic cat.

What? You ask. What? You want to go out? Well you can't.

You hear a chime.

It is your former employer informing you that they cannot release

your husband's password due to the Privacy Policy.

It is their 98th autoreply.

You bite your hand.

You check in on your husband.

After your husband went on roam, you received one message from him:

I am by a pond and a coyote is eating a frog. It's amazing.

You decide to go outside.

You walk to the public park.

There is a track where people run while watching whatever

they're watching.

You sit on an oversized bench.

You think of your old town house with the oatmeal sofa

before you and husband downgraded to this neighborhood.

The sofa made you happy.

You decide you need to keep up appearances.

You need to clip your husband's nails. They are getting long.

A strangled yip escapes from you and a jogger stares at you.

You see a palm tree and it is carved up with little phallic drawings.

You make a sound like tut-tut.

You enhance the park.

You fill in the balding grass and rub the offensive drawings

from the tree. You add coconuts.

You feel your insides are being squeezed out through a tiny hole

the size of a mosquito bite.

You hear children laughing as they rush out of a bus and it sounds

far away and watery, like how it used to in the movies, when the light was haloey,

and it was slow-motion, and the actor was having a terrible flashback.

But you are not having a flashback.

Underneath the sound of children laughing, you hear users chatting

over each other, which all blurs into a warring shadow of insects

and the one that sounds like a hornet is your husband,

telling you to put his stuff in storage.

Or sell it to pay off bills or

leave, why don't you goddamn leave.

You sit on the bench until the sky turns pink.

When your former employer let you go,

they said, you are now free to pursue what you want to pursue.

So here you are.

THE GOLDEN STATE

Here you are deep
inside the marrow of song
      a spirit shape tucked
in my ear before snow

streams an old-time town
      a general store selling cornmeal
      and used dentures
what time zone is this

home of sad marvels,
      pluck my memory out,
I am just immigrant enough
      to feel shame

for my overseas kin who live inside gaming
and still their warriors are listless,
      brooding
you cannot speak

      her brimmed mind
she went hysterically blind
      so they implanted an ocularis
and she said I see light
sharpening

to contours, a field,
marigolds, asters, golden poppies,
      I see their names
but why do I smell smoke

in the engine, the way memory
        will just hit
I unvalve the escape hatch
        a gentle hiss

breathing in a remote dark
        planet, suck in,
come back.

An obliterating heat. Or weather. How these other forces impede a post-war architecture's modernist aims. Similarly. I want to write out, one after another, a sequence of degraded colonial forms. My work engages the colony at the instant of maternal death. Part of being a writer is the capacity to make statements like this, privately. Is the colony a kind of mother? I want to study form as an activity of incarnation: the thing that abates, progresses but never loops again. Instead, I want to write my subjects to the end point and beyond, even if that means I am a failed British novelist of some kind. *BAN* is a novel of the race riot, for example, set in the U.K. The pre-biology—notes for a novel never written—extends from a World Conference of Cultural Psychiatry, to which I was a delegate, to the street on which "Ban"—a girl walking home from school in the opening moments of a riot—lies down to die. I am interested in social death and the acoustics of violence. I write historical fiction with verve.

from **BAN**

ARCHITECTURE AND PSYCHOSIS: [Notebook decompressions: World Association of Cultural Psychiatry: Congress 3]: London, March 2012 // Delhi-London-Denver: May 2012 [Notebook decompressions: Tate Modern, Chandigarh Architecture Museum, Denver Museum of Contemporary Art]

1. The effect of the built environment (prisons/neighborhood structures) on rates of affective and reactive psychosis.

Is the patient an ultra rapid CYP2D6 metabolizer? Why is accountability more often undiminished and less often diminished in the black and ethnic minority populations?

A black man (citizen) or black man from other part of Europe (non-citizen) or black African man (citizen or non-citizen) is three times more likely to be indicted of a crime; similarly, why is compulsory admission to a psychiatric facility 6% versus 2.6% in the local white population?

What if a patient has a decreased capacity to process certain compulsory medications? (See: BME populations). (Also: CYP2D6 allele frequency in Curaçao.)

Who assesses the pre-trial reports that might result in compulsory admission to a psychiatric facility?

Singh 2007: British Journal of Psychiatry: BME patients disproportionately detained under the Mental Health Act. See: The killing of Jonathon Zito by Christopher Koomis on the 24th of March, 2009. Track: Koomis care history and diagnosis. Consider: misdiagnosis, discrimination, differences in illness expression as related to higher psychosis rates in BME populations.

"The extremes of the spectrum are increasing."—The beautiful, extremely young Dutch psychiatrist in an ill-fitting pale yellow linen suit who starts to sweat as he shouts this last thing out, just before his study of the Dutch prison system and an analysis of the psychosis rates of the Dutch native, Turkish, Moroccan, Surinamese, Antillean and other non-western populations gets the biggest take-down of the conference.

I left the building to sit on the cemetery steps. This is the NOVO cemetery, an early immigrant Spanish and Portuguese (Jewish) cemetery in Mile End, surrounded now by the campus buildings of Queen Mary's College.

My mother used to teach art, music and poetry in primary schools almost entirely comprised of non-native children, both in Mile End and Bethnal Green. She'd wake at 4 a.m. to make the unleavened dough for our evening chapatis. Then, in tennis shoes, a sari and a black and white fake fur coat, she'd commute on the Metropolitan Line to Liverpool Street, where she'd change to the Central line. Her nickname was Demented Panda. Because of what she wore. Who she was. Her height. Her weight. Her way in the world. Her hands.

2. The plaques are pristine. They are made of a milky, hygienic marble.

The medical building glitters in the pale silver rain coming off the Thames. A non-wave. Evaporation. Hockney's California transposed to a London afternoon. From the hospital I went to the Tate and saw the Hockney. My friend once saw Hockney unloading his paintings from the back of a car in Santa Barbara, outside the art museum.

It was pouring with rain. I pushed open a gate and walked down to the Thames—afraid to slip, yet enchanted—by its roaring waves. The Thames is a tidal river. It is pewter, slate, violet—all the colors of the top-down world. From the Thames I went back to the hospital. Hospitals refract their contents; they are not built to retain illnesses, but to dispel them.

Document the corridor. Cure the corridor.

Hockney elevates then sections the medical building, an activity that also gives intense pleasure: to whom?

So love the pink, blank sky. And the palms.

3. There was pink lightning. I let it stop me.

Kindness—a radical milk—nourished me as I approached the step beneath the July green, the paragraph.

A longing for the sea, for salt seas—replaced some of my cells, the ones in my forearms, the ones that die off before they are ever seen.

I used up my stored energy, the creativity reserved for the novel. In the Stein collection, I removed the paintbrush from my hair and lay down on a bench beneath a geometric nude. I was investigating the sharp border between comedy and tragedy, and so I lay there for a few minutes, on my side, Ban-like, unobserved by the guard.

Later that summer, in Los Angeles, I got into the red sack. There on the butcher's table I turned around. I was naked and that amount of naked does something to a person. It wasn't a shop; it was a house.

All the doors are open to the rain.

Ban fulfills the first criterium of monstrosity simply by degrading: by emitting bars of light from her teeth and nails, when the rain sweeps over her then back again.

I like how the rain is indigo, like a tint that reveals the disease process in its inception.

Is Ban a monster? Yes. I can say yes, but I have to mean it. These are notes to accompany a decision that someone else has already made.

Who put her on the wet ground? It was gold and silver. It curled. Above her, the pink lightning was branched—forked—in five places. Sulphur, air, trees.

Boys. The boys scatter and sometimes they are men. A man.

A brown ankle on a crisp morning in the forest.

Ban: undone.

4. A successful plagiarist incorporates content to such an extent that when the content provider engages this content they feel guilty or weirdly on the offensive! That's all I have today on that: the monster that is as a creature in constant motion, devouring everything in its path: fur, plastics, things long-dead. The wake of such movement is a charnel ground.

My uncle and I once went to Rishikesh. I stayed back at the country lodge, reading Tolstoy on the covered porch; he, at night, went to the bone pit by the river and meditated until dawn. These practices have carried over into my life as an experimental writer in the continental United States.Often, I squat on a content.

I visualize the content as a heterogenous cone or mass. Like salt.

Or sugar. The plagiarist squats on the sugar, displacing the sugar into a singular mound of content. I think of all the cups of tea I could have drunk!

I once prevented myself from eating sugar by imagining that an elderly pedophile was squatting above it (the sugar), to urinate. That did the trick. See: inflammation and the immune system. It is impossible to take revenge upon the actual plagiarist; as a crime, conceptual plagiarism—the plagiarism of ideas and combinations of ideas or "unusual structures"—is notoriously hard to prove. Thus, by taking care of the toxic load in the body itself, the content provider is able to practice effective self-care in another, yet related, area.

In a labyrinth programmed to devour, the plagiarist would be sitting at a desk behind a privet hedge, typing.

But sometimes I want the labyrinth to be real: earth art on a warm-cool scale.

5. I want to have sex with what I want to become.

6. Architecture and Psychosis (2)

Yesterday, in the Chandigarh Architecture Museum, an homage to Le Corbusier complete with faded originals of his correspondence with Nehru, I saw (in an out of the way corner) this fantastic thing, the Hyperbolic-Paraboloid Dome of Assembly.

I thought immediately of the Wertheim coral reef that is crocheted in the hyperbolic plane. I asked Margaret Wertheim about schizophrenia and the brain, during a crochet workshop at the Denver Museum of Contemporary Art. She said or did not say: the topology of the schizophrenic brain is hyperbolic. I am simplifying the conversation, but it is remarkable to me that here in India I have found a third iteration of the term.

The museum makes me ecstatic.

I spent long summers in this city as a child, a Corbusean city block in which "the endless rhythms of balconies and louvres on its long facade are punctuated by asymmetry... geometry... the texturique." (Le Corbusier's planning notes.)

Corbusean fragments from letters (to Nehru, then the prime minister of India) and from other planning materials, blueprints or sketches. I wrote them down in my notebook, squinting in some cases to read the red or blue ink that had almost faded from view:

"I communicate this to you without any comments."

"My wish? Is that no reduction should be made concerning the Architect's office and especially not without beheadings!"

"It was a battle of space, fought within the mind. Arithmetic, texturique, geometrics: it would all be there when the whole was finished. For the moment, oxen, cows and goats, driven by peasants, crossed the sun scorched fields."

"Monuments: a) Open Hand, b) Tower of Shadows, c) Geometrical Wall, d) Martyr's memorial."

"The modular gives two series of harmonious dimensions based on the human body."

"The Edict of Chandigarh: a brief set of instructions for posterity."

Excellent sub-title for Ban or any other novel written by myself or another person: "a brief set of instructions for posterity."

I saw the tapestry designed and woven by le Corbusier for the Capitol building, replete with lightning bolt, cobra and inverted red triangle: symbols of tantra.

How the post-war city is spatialized, augmented and designed against the fold: an idea that collapses by 1992, at the point that weather systems corrode the concrete forms or blemish them, making the edict's harmony or comedic tone an anachronism without end.

Le Corbusier wasn't thinking.

About the water.

Or the terrible and obliterating heat.

JOHN KEENE

The best summation of my poetics lies in my poems "MO: Poesis," or "Self," or, rather, in their respective final lines: "Whom will I gather, gather into these folds," and "In the end, refuse signature." More broadly, though, my poetics comprises a search for what lies within the folds of languages, of experiences, in the languages of experience and the experiences of life, art, language. Here ethics, aesthetics, and the politics of the poetic strive to come together—whether they do or not. The poems offer and are what remains: the black, queer residue.

COLOR

To resort to other expressive methods, other ways of deriving the called thing, drawing. Without you. Through color the key, the eyes the harmonies, the soul palette with its innumerable stirrings. Can it be trapped as a figure, the perceptual color. Is it clear where the color space lies, where string and range begin. Without you, whether the fingers that play are representable, the fingers that say: artist. One layer beside another, differentiable, where tendency is evident, one key or another, the graphic that enfolds, withholds. From closing to stitching. Vibrations as color. Touching drawing. Compact or not compact, call things soul, represent them as differentiable. Where it is clearest is lyrical, where it passes through itself as connections, figures mass. Without you, the other ways, through methods tying the spectrum to what stays, what plays beneath the other layers, untying the last one. Without keys or harmonies. And where would it be, without you?

(ANTI-)KANTIAN

Injuring it, when I look.

What am I opening?

Unlocking or loosing movement, the query of intent.

To enter the fail, the medium falling

                in marks and strokes, the filter through

           as though the afterimage captured

                      synthetic, not ideal forms.

You can say that it came about of listening to some essence

        and function, the fall through conscious

               and mechanical, pictured being.

Why?

Failure. Looking in, how when I filter the frail margin

              record of ideal forms of something

       so mundane and readymade

            moment ravels there.

Mapping sources captures something different.

Does that tell me much about itself?

Another question: medium, set, space strategy.

Is it crucial to know, know how?

Metal or mechanical key, pen and pencil

      or you could say memory, erasure,

             mettle structures felt design.

Entering it, what you used to trap

              and draw up as transitory,

        trying to reveal, the result more or less.

How drawing ultimately

        is coming into forms,

     how looking

  (for) recreates

    deforms.

MO: POEISIS

Thinking, and wondering how to stutter: poetry. Thinking and wondering how desires armor her, how the paper and fold are position, yearning. In public as quiet, without power or armor, the backs of her poems struck silent, stuck and lost so... or scooping up and working that, out of shy and felt and separate. How do they stand? To dedicate myself, to message and process after talking. Do that, I didn't do that. To shear poetry, share it. Little notes on the backs of her promise, opening, a fierce circle of thinking up front. Present-ing. Things found, written on the screen, on presence itself. Thinking wheels. Writing. The group, conceptual as art is, shit peeped yet never said before, her thing—things—think. To role, to have a roll, going all hard and realing, paper reels and sticks in there imagination lies. All that in one place? On it, onto it, in it. Whom will I gather, gather into these folds?

AFTER C (3):TAYLORIANA

I have to find it again, an extreme music. Inspired by voicings: out, but I may lose it again. That I may live it, utterly beautiful in its rendering. The brink of composition, brink of the hand called looking. And open, drawing like flying open alone, broken without having to take me. Musically it was composition of a distant whiteness, where absence too was thrown, by concentration alone, but not in the listening. Drawing. A profound transitional, kaleidoscopic, where the axes of decay were really the depiction. Dark seisms really come to mind, the first death and the last one, each darker, these first, these powerful, arranged as a collection. Arranged, not solo. At that time I was collecting other pieces, hands, the electronic composed as an album. Looking as some other thing. But I may pick another break, piece the track. In concert. I've since thrown it. He called the depth extraordinary. A fearful copy.

HOW TO DRAW A BUNNY

for Ray Johnson and Nayland Blake

Drawing a bunny requires at a minimum a pencil and some paper.

Talking about the bunny or talking about drawing the bunny is not the same as drawing the bunny.

Drawing a bunny requires only three strokes if you capture the ears in only one.

Drawing a bunny requires only a modicum of will.

When you are drawing a bunny, try not to talk about drawing a bunny.

When you are drawing a bunny, try not to think about drawing a bunny.

When you are drawing a bunny, try not to think about drawing a pussy or a cock.

The bunny may be male or female, or no gender at all, so long as it's a bunny.

The bunny may be black or white or gray or fluorescent, or any color or no color at all, and drawn in thirteen or more ways, so long as it's a bunny and not a blackbird.

Drawing a bunny is unlikely to make you rich or popular, or the subject of extensive gossip or scholarly discussion, except among those who care about drawing, bunnies, and drawing bunnies.

Drawing a bunny doesn't mean that you have drawn the true bunny, or the false bunny, just that you have drawn the bunny.

Just because you've drawn the bunny doesn't mean you know the bunny.

Just because you've drawn the bunny doesn't mean you do not know the bunny.

The bunny, as idea or image, need not carry any metaphysical weight.

The bunny, as idea or image, can nevertheless still function perfectly well as a trope or metaphor.

Speaking about the bunny as "beautiful" introduces a host of philosophical problems.

The drawn bunny may or may not be undrawing itself, which is for someone else to discern.

The half-drawn bunny is not the same as the drawn, partially drawn or undrawn bunny.

Drawing a bunny is not the same as drawing a puppy, or a kitten, unless you designate them rigidly under the name of "bunny."

Why draw a bunny when you can draw a pony, or a tank, or a dollar sign?

Why draw a bunny when you can draw bathwater, or compounded interest, or .57 Magnum?

Why draw a bunny or dollar sign when you can draw up your own will?

To erase a bunny requires only three strokes.

Drawing a bunny can be emotional or unemotional, though the effect is usually evaluative.

Drawing a bunny has a number of purposes, the chief of which is drawing a bunny.

Drawing a bunny requires no originality, even if your livelihood or sense of self and authenticity hinge on it.

Drawing a bunny requires no philosophy, though you and the bunny may be of a philosophical bent.

Drawing a bunny doesn't depend upon your dreaming a bunny, though it's best if you draw before you dream.

The dream bunny will never be the drawn bunny, since the artwork is always the death-mask of its conception.

Drawing a bunny requires no talent, even though you may put great stock in artistic genius.

Drawing a bunny requires a modicum of concentration, even though you might put no stock in artistic technique.

Drawing a bunny is like learning a language, only it takes considerably less time.

Drawing a bunny can occur anywhere you can draw a bunny.

Drawing a bunny saves no one, though at the very least the bunny is drawn.

Drawing a bunny only requires three strokes, though the effect can be abstract, representational, or conceptual, or some median between the three.

Drawing a bunny says about you only that you drew a bunny, and nothing about your intellect or character.

Drawing a bunny successfully will make you want to draw another bunny.

Drawing a bunny unsuccessfully will make you want to draw another bunny.

Drawing a bunny requires only a pencil or similar writing instrument and some paper.

Drawing, undrawing or withdrawing a life requires a lifetime.

CONFIDENCE IN TALK

An aphorism from Ben Jonson's *Timber, or Discoveries* says that "language most shows a man: speak, that I may see thee." That could be the motto of personal style: my voice produces an image of me. In fact, my voice is the best possible image; it "most shows" me. My sentences could all be lies, but my voice can't help telling the truth. The concept of personal style is based on an incredible confidence in talk. You can see that confidence in Jonson's poems and plays, especially his interest in terms of art. Each character comes with a dictionary, a grammar, a tone, a rhythm. An extreme example of this would be Nockem's tendency to replace every word with "vapours." The hallmark of a style is that it can be imitated, but styles in Jonson remain the signatures of particular characters even when other characters pick them up. When Mistress Overdo complains about her husband's "enormities," that word still belongs to Adam Overdo. "Mine own words turned against me like swords!"

Compare Gertrude Stein in "Composition as Explanation": "Everybody knows it because everybody says it." That could be the motto of period style. All the moderns are working on the same problem, using the same tools. Her aphorism declares a confidence in talk that is at least as incredible as Jonson's. The temptation would be to reverse her formula: nobody knows it because everybody says it. How well does what "everybody says" represent what anyone knows? Received ideas aren't knowledge, are they? For Stein, what "everybody says" represents the deepest, most valuable kind of knowledge because no one has to think about it.

Jonson and Stein trust the sounds of their voices. I'm a shy person. I have no confidence in talk. Especially my talk.

I talk too quietly and too quickly, sometimes so quickly that my mouth accidentally makes a kissing or smacking sound between words. I don't have a lot of control over what happens to my voice, and there is occasional slurring, stammering, odd emphasis, and even breaking. Unless I'm thinking about it and trying not to do it, my eyes compulsively snap shut when I open my mouth.

So that's what I have to work with. And in a sense I realize that this is partly a kind of personal myth, a story I tell about myself that maybe used to be true but doesn't quite match the person I have become. I mean, I'm a lot better than I was fifteen years ago, but still! My voice is a constant reminder of the limitations of my ability to transform myself. I'm confident in writing. I feel that I can be basically anything in writing. But when I talk, I'm stuck with inferior tools, and there isn't much I can do with them. I expect to be humiliated in speech, but not in writing. This is probably why I became a writer.

If I ever made a conscious decision to become a writer, it was in September 1991. What happened then was that I realized that writing and talking are very different. That was how I formulated it. In fact they aren't so different—they include, blend, and change into each other in lots of ways. I just relate to them differently. Talking is my way of suffering. It's humiliation and difficulty, and I have no confidence in it. Whereas writing is, if not exactly easy or fluent—"There is always something wrong with writing," according to Denton Welch—at least it's usable and shapeable. Talking, I can't get words to do anything; writing, I'm actually quite confident in my ability to make words do things. That's what artistry is: the ability to do anything in a medium. But because writing and talking are so closely linked, because they use similar materials and feed back into each other, I don't think my writing ever communicates a sense of mastery or joy in the liberation of language from difficulty. Instead it vividly remembers all the humiliations of being unformed. This probably becomes clear when I turn it into speech by reading it out loud.

THE SORE THROAT

I'm inventing a machine
for concealing my desire.
And I'm inventing another
machine for concealing the
machine. It's a two-machine
system, and it sounded like
laughter. And I'm inventing
a machine for concealing
the sound. You, to me: "Why are
you concealing the beauty
of your machine?" Every machine
has more beauty than the last,
for everything whose purpose
is to conceal seems to change,
in the end, into a sign
of what it's concealing. And
now the sound that once sounded
like laughter is so loud that
it seems more like sobbing or
laughter concealing sobbing.
All my inventing is a
complete disaster. It's not
concealing my desire, it's
talking about my desire
to conceal my desire, like
a voice on a message machine
that would say: "Hello. About
desire, I'd like to say a
word or two. It's not your eyes,
it's not the word you say, it's
not your complaining voice that
I desire. All I desire

is your applause." It's hard not
to hear what the message is
saying, also it's hard to
keep myself from inventing
another machine to keep
from hearing it. So invent
a machine for disinventing.
This will be the last machine
I ever invent, and its
purpose will just be to change
every machine into shit.
No more inventing (for me).

—What a shame. It once was a
wonder of a machine; now
it's more like a disaster.

—I think he left a message . . .

—You're wrong: he just left a mess.

'WORDS' 'AND' 'FLESH'

I'm Chiquita Banana. My
Name is taken from the shop where
I was made. "I" have a lot of
Words in "my" head
That "I" don't say. "I" love "the" warmth
"Of" "the" candle

And "I" also enjoy its light.
"Of" course "I" sometimes do misspeak
"The" meaningful "words in my head."
If "I" should let
"My" voice go, what obscenities
"I" might utter!

We can never entirely sleep
"And" sex, as everyone knows, "is"
Mostly dormant. "The" library
"Is" "a" sexy
Place since "the" books on "the" shelves are
"Mostly dormant."

Being "a" poet means "that" "I"
Am not constrained to make "sex" "from"
"My" own obdurate flesh alone.
"I" also have
Opportunities "to make sex"
Out "of" "words" "and"

Concepts. Therefore, "as" "a poet"
Even "I might" be considered
"Sexy." "The" ingredients "of"
"My" "being" "are"

"Words" "and" "flesh" "mostly." "Everyone"
Has "the" same "flesh"

Only "the" "words" "are" different.
"A" recovered "name" suddenly
Floods "the" memory "taken from
The shop where I
Was made." "I" once gave someone "a"
Dictionary.

STUPID PRETENDING TO BE
SMART COULD BE SMARTER THAN SMART
PRETENDING TO BE STUPID

DOROTHEA LASKY

My beliefs about what makes poetry a special form of writing stem from a deep appreciation of the sublime beauty of everyday language, which can be, of course, the speech of both written and spoken text. I truly believe that poetry's value is that it seeks to sum up, represent, concoct, conjure, and connect the voices that have lived and died among us, but have not always had the opportunity to have a voice. In this way, poetry is always a human thing, in that it is always seeking the human voice among us. What a poet does is to make clear how this language might contain music and then turns this language into its own kind of music. How a poet does this is not really a mystery (and thus, is always past a conversation regarding "the muse"), but involves a set of filters and circumstances (in their own way systematically complex) that fuel the poet's ability to be able to listen to the music of everyday speech, and then require his or her own openness to reconfigure this into its own set of sounds. How we train poets is very important to my poetics, this set of filters and circumstances, because to me poetry should be most concerned with making more of itself. It is its own lack of preciousness with which it gets its strength. To sum it up, poetry is special to me because it is a set of voices that are neverending, that are so past the idea of the singular that an I always contains an ineffable spark, or really because, as Jack Spicer says, "Poetry ends like a rope."

I HAD A MAN

Today when I was walking
I had a man tell me as he passed
That I was a white bitch (he was white)
And to not look at him
Or he was going to 'fuck me in my little butthole'
I wandered away
Who is to say
I think I am a white bitch
My butt is big
But I believe my butthole is little
This violence that we put on women
I don't think it's crazy
Someone I know said
'Oh, that man was crazy'
I don't think he was crazy
Maybe he could tell I had a look in my eye
That wasn't crazy anymore
Maybe he could feel the wild cool blood in me
And it frightened him
And he lashed out in fear
Maybe he knew I was the same as him
But had been born with this kind face and eyes
Doughlike appurtenances
What about the day I left
What happened then
Still I'm glad he said that to me
Still I'm glad he was so cruel to me
What bitter eye knew I had a voice
To say what men have done to me
What unkind wind has blown thru my brain
To make me speak for the wretched
To speak wretchedly about the ugly
To make my own face ugly and simple
To contort this simple smile into a haunting song

I LIKE WEIRD ASS HIPPIES

I like weird ass hippies
And men with hairy backs
And small green animals
And organic milk
And chickens that hatch
Out of farms in Vermont
I like weird ass stuff
When we reach the other world
We will all be hippies
I like your weird ass spirit stick that you carry around
I like when you rub sage on my door
I like the lamb's blood you throw on my face
I like heaping sugar in a jar and saying a prayer
And then having it work
I like cursing out an enemy
And then cursing them in objects
Soaking their baby tooth in oil
Lighting it on fire with a tiny plastic horse
I like running through the fields of green
I am so caught up in flowers and fruit
I like shampooing my body
In strange potions you bought wholesale in Guatemala
I like when you rub your patchouli on me
And tell me I'm a man
I am a fucking man
A weird ass fucking man
If I didn't know any better I'd think I were Jesus or something
If I didn't know any better I'd sail to Ancient Greece
Wear sandals
Then go to Rome
Murder my daughter in front of the gods
Smoke powdered lapis
Carve pictographs into your dress
A thousand miles away from anything

When I die I will be a strange fucking hippie
And so will you
So will you
So get your cut-up heart away from
What you think you know
You know, we are all going away from here
At least have some human patience
For what lies on the other side

ME AND THE OTTERS

Love makes you feel alive

Johnny my animal you have no idea

How beautiful you are to me in the morning

When it is 5 a.m. and I am lonely

Everyone is dying around me

I eat spinach bread to keep my sanity, I am

Like Lisa in the mental unit with my father

I am Muriel who throws tables

I play blackjack with the clowns

Oh yes I do all that for a salad

Your black hair is better than a piece of fate

I find in the sky when I am looking

45,000 miles above the earth

For things that make it all worthwhile

I do this for you but you will never know

How dear you are to me

You chop leaves in your house in New York City

Dream of glamorous women and even too they are great

No one will ever love you like I do that is certain

Because I know the inside of your face

Is a solid block of coal and then it too

Something that is warm like warm snow

I hold the insides of you in my palm

And they are warm snow, melting even

With the flurries glutted out of the morning

When I get on the plane the stewardess tells me to let loose

My heart, the man next to me was the same man as last week

Whoever those postmodernists are that say

There is no universal have never spent any time with an animal

I have played tennis with so many animals

I can't count the times I have let them win

Their snouts that were wet with health

Dripping in the sun, then we went and took a swim
Just me and the otters, I held them so close
I felt the bump of ghosts as I held them.
There is no poem that will bring back the dead
There is no poem that I could ever say that will
Arise the dead in their slumber, their faces gone
There is no poem or song I could sing to you
That would make me seem more beautiful
If there were such songs I would sing them
O they would hear me singing from here until dawn

EVER READ A BOOK CALLED AWE?

Have you ever read a book called *AWE*?
I have. I wrote it. That's my book.
I wrote that book. I wrote that one.
Some people read it, they said,
We will make your book.
I said, Really? I love you.
They said, We love you, too.
I said, Good then
I will love you forever
They said, Great!, and looked scared
Some people I love
Don't love me
Others love me
That's good
When you sit in landscape of snow
And you're a bird, that's Awe
When you look over a big green field
And the dead soldiers lay all around you, that's Love
That's Love and Awe.
Say it
That's Love and Awe.
There is nothing better.
Or if there is
Then I don't care

TORNADO

I remember he was bent down
Like a whirlpool
I was yelling at him
He looked scared and backed away
Another time, I squinted my eyes to see
And he said I looked ugly
The funny part was when
My sister asked me where he went to
And I just didn't know
He just disappeared one day into nothing
I am rotting and rancid
Each day, rotting, but I am water, too
I am a watery nymph that is hot and wet
Like a wetted beast
I saw the man walking, hunched over
And thought it was him
"Father!" I yelled after the man
Who was hunched, he was going somewhere
He turned but the face was green
It is a black life, but I don't want to die
I don't want to die, I don't ever want to die
Goddamn you, don't you shoot me in my sleep
Let me rot on this earth forever
Like a carrot I will be everything God can't see
Oh what do I mean
God can see everything
I mean the angels, I mean the half-gods
I mean the flowers, don't ever let them see me live forever
Don't you ever let them see
That I am all root here in the ground

I've noticed that John Ashbery uses the word magic a lot in his poems. In *Three Poems*, for example, Ashbery writes something like, "there is still magic in the world." That is how I remember the poem, anyway, offering testimony, despite its wide, expansive reticence. It may seem like a rather mundane statement, and individual lines in Ashbery's writing always trace a fine line between inspired and mundane, roving between the eventual and the apocalyptic. Ashbery's point, I think, is to remind us that, despite the overwhelming atomization of everyday life, openings happen, signs of reversal in the air, traces of someone else's circumference making an impact. Poetry reminds us that we are among collections, groupings, readings. Poems can open up a lot of territory in our everyday lives. Any poem will open up a wide terrain, giving us words and giving us permission, affectively, conceptually, rhetorically, spiritually, theoretically, persuasively, magically. Any word can open an extensive and epic amount of landscape or implication, as Hart Crane's poems demonstrate. Or H.D.'s. By looking elsewhere, I try to write against my tendencies. To be open to the elements and open to the margins. This is not easy. History and language exert an enormous pressure, but they also offer endless resources for experience. Spending time at the limit of someone else's thinking can be very enabling. I look for permission elsewhere. If I look sideways away from myself, if I disfigure myself, I may find something. My own mortality, for example. A sigh of relief, escaping.

H.D.

Become a pilot of an arc

see a spider for good luck

What falls by accident

is an arrival

What falls is elegant

wind in ink

Her gentle vocal storms

supply all anthems

vivid in frets or garlands

HART CRANE

I am alive I am not alive
I am falling up
in my dreams
or I am dreaming
I gave back the stars
for a living
I was braided
to survive
I was an usher
a first impression
of Atlantic sounds
New Amsterdam
floating in space
eating the skin of wool
I saw circles
I heard zero
count to zero
I was
ecstatic deliverance
of everyday life
I bathed in it
I wanted to have written it
and was catapulted
into the last
living detail
at the beginning
at the end

MAGIC SHELL

What a boon to find a word
on two ends of an egg
that has lost
its nerve its language and elision
I never learned
to speak out loud
I remember
I don't remember
in a film we share
we put a dress on the cat
we carry the house
and fake sleep inside
Jurassic flowers under delta flowers
summer pulled all the halos
I wrote in the air long lemonade
with baroque legs
a song
a very long tally
and a magic cake

FLANNEL BELLS

Who knows why the novel begins with joy and ends in failure. Who learns the truth first curries mutiny among the melons, whispers in a simple pretext for the world. That's a floating cell in the wind. Flannel ridges of the mind, flannel bells repose. Two parabolic orbits in the dirt, it remains to publish time.

INERT SAVOIR

It is difficult to fold a minute with the beloved. Do not enter. Land becomes like chintz that swallows, a tempered line of bougainvillea. Every tear is great, every corner of the mouth that gives to others. What vague taps and zippered fears that swell. Another torn skirt. Another glass. Another government of water.

RACHEL LEVITSKY

"(Yes, only fragments are angry!)"

—Heribierto Yépez, *Wars. Threesomes. Drafts. & Mothers*

There are many things I think about myself as a writer. I don't like to say too much about myself as a writer. I sink with the feeling that to begin with the predicate "I am" means constructing a mythology or a stranglehold. Mythology is context, as stranglehold; something to reproduce voice, pattern, deny the changing air outside. But the reason for this text, *The Story of My Accident Is Ours*, a "novel" I say of it, was to write something about the shiftiness of the present time—particularly shifty because it is a time yet much responded to in novel form. By that I mean that form must itself reflect the instability of our moment, which is built on a mountain of junk, literal, strewn plastic, a landscape defined by loss without narrative trace (see Miranda Mellis' *The Revisionist*). What can be gained there, politically, toward the future. I was happy when I *landed* the form also because it was an excuse for me to write some essay-fiction-polemic/political-tract-experimental prose in which I could narrate things I'd done and seen and thought about over time, activist time. And yet to be a poet? Sonically lyric(ish), lacking the specificity required by the already-form of fiction; things written around (circularly) to be familiar but not named only pointed to; identification therefore mutable, mobile, shifty; novel because of plot device, not plot: *My Accident*; "*The Story Of*" not a story that is told but a story about telling. How to. How to not. How to not tell as though I am speaking; how to be both extremely condensed and a quick read, populist even, made easy by rhythm I wish. Not in order to be shaped difficult. Only excessive to extreme, an attempt to control excessive in the extreme, to contain lots of junk. And wanting inside, beyond the gravitas, humor. And queer, and jewish. Too. And/but more secondary in this book, the surface funny, more inside joke. The problem of *telling* any however you slice it, if one is a poet. According to Yépez, *telling* being controlling, not angry like the fragment. *Revenge* according to lesbian, novelist, activist Sarah Schulman, a la Abigail Child, who received this when lovers with. Not unhinged, emotionally unstable, "affirmation in negation," which is poetry defined by Susan Howe in *My Emily Dickinson*. Not necessarily gendered but necessarily coming from it so.

171

FROM ALMOST ANY ANGLE

We woke into the world—

All at once and all one way like characters you'd see in a science fiction movie, without parents, cloned for the purpose of replacing the organs of the rich, or jailed indefinitely and repeatedly for our childbearing ability. We had the appearance of arriving whole, the sets of our features predetermined and complete.

Defined by limitation—

We were kept away from history by serial clearances: slums, streets, the poor, then the rich, then the home, then the street, then the neighborhood, then the mall, and then the mall. (The mall.)

We recognized each other—

We communicated by way of a vacant look in our eyes and sophistication in our speech when we had the energy to speak. We were not quite like creatures in zombie movies that were popular again in our time. We didn't join in the common cause of destroying one another, or making another more like us. We lacked killer instinct. We doubted the necessity, that what we were should be reproduced or multiplied. We were ignorant of what we were, uncertain about the ways we did have, what they were and how they'd come to be.

What we knew better than what we were and the ways we had was all that we were strange to. We were strange to the ways of smiles—smiles possessed by the ones on television, big and radiant, infused with all the light in the room from which their image was cast, smiles worn by the ones outside in front of the church, placidly making their way through those who'd get in their way of smiling and smiles exchanged by the two who were passing each other, in a case where one is walking down a sidewalk and another is driving in order to deliver a package from a truck.

We did not intend to be unfriendly nor dour though I can see (now) we have often and legitimately been so perceived. At one point in time I imagine we could not have been perceived any other way. Left by ourselves we did not know how else to be. We were made, mostly, all one way.

AFTER IMAGE

The ground beneath us cannot be trusted; we need new ground. There is a history of art that is well known to us in our times, of found objects reconfigured because although the past is nearly universally understood to be destructive as a force left to itself we find it impossible to retire. Rather than wrestle with its unruly enormity, we resign ourselves to picking up its pieces, though often, we throw them right back down.

Some, those we consider visionaries, collect these ejected pieces off city streets in order to rearrange them into small monuments which become passing moments for passersby who wait with uncertainty for the light to change, who momentarily pause to recall the author-makers of these found and finding visual narratives as they rehear a story in the head, one the radio told, a long story including details of life and death, thereby causing the passersby, us or any of the others of us who pass us by on these same corners equally regularly, find ourselves listening to and find the calm, possessed, evenly spoken voice so very widely broadcast in our times, as it recounts this tale of inspiration and woe, implying not only the one but the many other invisible others like the one about whom the story is so... if not thoroughly then tellingly told, who make as these author-makers make, leading us to wonder, no... to worry... about how they are doing and if they are living and if they might be well and if it is possible that they are going to be okay, which seems improbable now that we can see, no... hear... that the work they make is experienced like this, like a *reminder*, rather than as than a fact for itself.

Finding these fragments, broken pieces for which we ourselves serve in the role of agents for spreading, can be the cause of a change in course so that instead of fully reaching the spot that is designated as home a walk is taken around the block. There was no *actual* thought that we would find him, but we imagine that we *might*—*little* is truly impossible, still, for there is *park*.

THE LOVER

To look at a lover from any angle is the meaning of love. I am restating something Picasso said when I say that beauty is monumental when the absurd grotesque of one angle meets in forceful equality the graceful dignity of another. In a lover that is being looked at from any angle these positions are mobile. This is the meaning of love. We are wary, in this case (for, we are wary in general), of parts that fit together too neatly. We cannot bear suffering without a show, a paroxysm. The paroxysm outsizes our container. Our container explodes. We refit accordingly. It can't be easy; I take it we must be born with or learn to develop strong hearts.

Still, we often feel as though we could die of this world; we often do.

Q: You began publishing as a poet, but your work increasingly tends to refuse traditional classifications. How unimportant is genre for what you're up to?

A: It's funny. I never really wanted to write something more than once, so that makes genre an interesting concept to inhabit for awhile before departing, and of course a door is an evocative thing. Genres are time sensitive—they wear out. When was the last time you read a bucolic by Theocritus? Or an eclogue? A menu in a restaurant wears out before the *amuse bouche* arrives, but a work of literature is regarded as something that takes a bit more time. But this is changing. I think works of literature should be structured more like RSS feeds or Yelp restaurant reviews, i.e. I am more interested in literature as a highly transient event rather than a timeless architectural structure, and most of my work has moved toward more diffuse forms of reading across a host of different platforms, and multiple genres, some of which are related to hardware and some to software. Literature has always been atmospheric and mood-based—I just wanted to do this more literally. Likewise, genres emerge out of mediums, and mediums absorb various genres. I mean what is *7CV* besides a book and what is *Bibliographic Sound Track*, which transpires in PowerPoint—quite a few other things are suggested. Are these works poetry, nonfiction or a novel? What is the minimum amount of information needed to codify a reading as genre-specific?

Q: When did you start incorporating visual art into your literary work?

A: About fifteen years ago, when I first started compiling a long prose work called *Our Feelings Were Made by Hand*. And then the PPT works and the films in Director are visual works that foreground long term, durational reading procedures or interactions. At a reading in the MoMA galleries, I read against Donald Judd's *Untitled 1976*. Language is a reflected thing surrounded by other reflected things. And the surface of a sculpture by Donald Judd, which was given a coat of very thin motorcycle paint, is prone to high fluorescence and deterioration. I was interested in the break down of nitrocellulose paints as they relate to the leakage (of descriptions) that is a text into a room, in this case, a conservation text (on a Judd sculpture restoration), along with a few plays by Kieran Daly and some poems by Frank Kuenstler. A poem is not much different from a faucet dripping in the room next door. Or a particular shade of paint that was a slightly different shade ten minutes or ten years ago.

This exchange is excerpted from "A Faucet Dripping in the Room Next Door: An Interview with Tan Lin by Eric Lorberer": http://blogs .walkerart.org/ecp/2013/03/27/interview-with-tan-lin/

from INSOMNIA AND THE AUNT

On March 10, I board a plane to Seattle, rent a white Honda Acura and drive eighty-seven miles to Concrete, Washington and the Bear Park Motel, a cheap motel on the western edge of North Cascades National Park that is run by a half-Chinese, half-English woman who happens to be my aunt. My aunt once told me that the rooms in the motel have seven foot ceilings and are lined with cinderblocks painted yellow. I have a few old photographs of this motel, most of which were sent to my mother, who thinks a motel in the middle of nowhere is some kind of crime against nature and has never visited, even though my aunt has extended numerous invitations on post cards. On the day before I leave, I show my mother a postcard of the motel and a photo of a woman in a cowboy hat. My mother glances at both and says, "I do not remember."

From a genealogical perspective, my aunt and uncle started their lives in America with a Chinese restaurant in Spokane and later in Seattle. Their first restaurant went out of business, they moved to Seattle to open another one, I think it was called Ming's Garden, but they got tired of serving people American Chinese food, so in the early '80s they decided to close the restaurant down and travel east, *into* the wilderness. They settled in a place near North Cascades National Park, near an Indian reservation. My aunt has always told me, in an inconsequential sort of grammatical inversion, that this is "the story of your lives" only backwards, from America to the real America, from China to somewhere you've never been before. And like most Orientals in the mid-seventies (or "Asian people" as they have been called since the mid-nineties), there was never the slightest bit of emotion on her face when she told me this story. Someone said "The Oriental, we are good at killing emotions," and I think that person was right.

459:—LAKE WASHINGTON PONTOON BRIDGE, SEATTLE, WASHINGTON

ONLY CONCRETE PONTOON BRIDGE IN THE WORLD.   47647

The drive from Seattle to Concrete takes me an hour and fifty minutes. It is late afternoon when I arrive. I pull into the spot in front of the lobby window and pull my bags from the trunk. My aunt is crying in front of the lobby window, which is back lit like a movie set. She runs out, yanks the duffel from my hands and bump drags it two or three steps in front of me to room seventeen, which is the room my aunt always takes me to whenever I visit, just as Salvador Dali when he came to New York always stayed at the St. Regis and always in room 1628. Whenever I visit during the next decade, my aunt will perform the same actions, with the same deliberate energy I associate with following a recipe one knows very well or watching re-runs on TV. She will cry in exactly the same manner, in front of the neon NO VACANCY sign in the window, with the same uncontrollable wailing and tears and half-Chinese words I do not understand. None of this I can hear very well through the glass. When I think of these actions, they give off, like the paradox surrounding a guess, the appearance of slightness inside moments that have already happened, as if my aunt's life were endlessly re-passing a single point in time, like an actor in a sitcom or a car going past the same highway exit night after night on its way home. And yet the repetition of my aunt's tears meant something completely different ten years after it first happened.

I don't remember much of this motel, but there is, as I gather from the post cards and photographs, an occasional painting in the rooms and once, when I first thought about visiting my aunt, when I was in high school, I remember seeing a photograph of a door that had been kicked in and which my aunt had pasted onto the back office wall. I don't know if this memory is based on something my aunt wrote me in a letter or said to me or whether I clipped the picture from a magazine many years later. The only photograph of my aunt that I have managed to hold onto through the years has her wearing a white cowboy hat and dark sunglasses that seem out of place in the wilderness, and that signal the sort of disruption or lie that I associate with Asians in the movies or in Ohio where I grew up, or Asians in fast food restaurants like McDonalds, where I have never eaten and where I have never seen a Chinese person eating. I have watched hundreds of movies with Asians and fake Asians in them, and the one thing that makes them all the same (except the white Asians) is that the Asians never stare into your eyes through the glass of a TV screen and you are never allowed to look too deeply into theirs. I think it is for this reason that whenever I think about my aunt, and TV for that matter, I can never remember my aunt's eyes (they appear to belong to someone else), and think instead of Robert Redford, who said in an interview that it is necessary for the body to lie to the mind (not the other way around) when acting and that the various strata of lying are continually searching for each other in the wilderness that most people call the truth and that my aunt calls television. For my aunt, TV can never really lie because it is on all the time, unlike the theatre, where there are all sorts of changes of scenery and which as a result goes on and off and is thus the perfect medium for telling lies one after another. But in my aunt's motel, the TV never goes off and all these changes are not changes at all; they're commercials.

For my aunt, and I think for Robert Redford, lying was a specific thing, like a baby crying in a room or an animal with a soul or, at the least, those mental states that scientists believe trigger particular actions like chasing after a bug or moving to another branch, which is to say that lying is the most sincere way of expressing oneself, and the best way anyone has of connecting one thing to another. As Paul Newman said, lying is a highly flirtatious and mechanical form that the body has of creating a gene pool. For this reason lying is never natural (in the reproductive sense)[1] and is best expressed with the eyes, whose motions are perceived to be distinct from the somaform and somatic expressions. Everyone thinks you can make love with your eyes but really the only thing you can do

with your eyes is lie with them. People who cry a lot tend to have more affairs than those who don't. Lying and having sex are best done with the eyes completely closed. To lie and have sex at the same time is one of the greatest things anyone can do. It is of course much harder to lie when staring directly at someone or something (like food) that one likes. It is impossible to lie to a computer that's turned off. A blank computer screen can still remind us of a face.

In the years since my aunt's death, I have often thought about what holds the parts of a family together, and I think it may be lies told in families almost like ours, or, in other words, American families in Ohio, not Chinese ones in Seattle. When we were growing up, my Chinese parents never told me much about my half-Chinese aunt, whether she

TAN LIN

was an aunt on my mother's or my father's side, whether she was a real aunt or just a Chinese auntie, or whether she was an American person who looked half Asian. I called her *kan-ma*. I am pretty sure *kan ma* means person related to a mother, even though *nai nai* and *wai po* are the words for grandmother on the father and mother's side respectively, and she was neither one of these. I think *kan* means *dry*, and so *kan ma* is probably a *dry mother* or one who doesn't nurse you. I never called her *a yi*, who I think was a real aunt on my mother's side and lived in New Jersey even though she was twenty years younger than my mother and a step-sister to her. My step-aunt's Chinese name was probably not quite actually hers, and likewise, my aunt's name is not quite right either. My mother called my aunt "Big Sister," and sometimes "Second Sister," none of which made much sense, as my mother has told my sister and me that she only had one sister, a half-sister, who was the daughter of her father and a second wife. Some names are simply too complicated or literal for American English, like a mother with no milk or an aunt who is not an aunt but is called one anyway. At any rate, when thinking of my aunt, I think of her at odd hours of the day or evening, like a television playing accidentally in another room, just as I think of my mother and father giving themselves American names when they arrived in Seattle. The names for my family are linked, like a mirror or perhaps a footnote, to the physical world and to social inconsistencies and historical accidents. In other words, my mother and father rarely saw my aunt in my presence, except maybe once on our first and only family visit to a Chinese restaurant in Spokane. Some relatives are meant to be imagined years before or after they died.

After my aunt checks in the last of the guests, I go see her in the front office. She rustles through the desk drawers and pulls out one can of Franco-American SpaghettiO's, one can of Chef Boyardee, two plastic bowls, a few plastic forks and a moist towelette. A white Toyota Camry and a grey Subaru are parked, tail in, towards the lobby window, just beyond the NO VACANCY sign. My aunt empties a can into an aluminum pot. What looks like a mom, dad, and two kids are pulling duffel bags and canoe paddles from a roof rack. Two kids are unloading the white car.

"The white one? " I ask.

"Teenagers."

"How old?"

My aunt shrugs. "Their license is almost expired. Ohio. Maybe as old as you."

I try to do the math in my aunt's English. "Car or them?"

My aunt shrugs. I recognize the shrug of someone who has been lied to.

180

"The Toyota?"

"A family called Bumas." My aunt switches channels and drops the remote in her lap. She points to something outside like something on TV.

"You mean the hatchback?"

"People from Queens."

My aunt, forgetting we are watching TV in America says, "*Hah. ge dong, si teou lie tyan. shia lie,*" instead of "*Nyyg dong. shi diaw de dih. shiah le,*" using the Paoting dialect she learned from her nanny when she was (Chinese) age seven, and which I do not speak.

I translate the words aloud, "That... thing... has... dropped.... to... the.... floor?" My aunt nods.

I nod back. The sun is setting. My aunt remembers more details, in Jewish English. "Shaskan. A dad. They have a tent and a wok. Rhoda."

"Who?" I squint into the window. "They look pale."

"They must be real," my aunt says, "with a name like that."

"Where are they going?" I ask.

"Camping," my aunt says. The taller boy drops a blue and white plastic cooler that has "Playmate" written on it. It hits the pavement and bounces against the Subaru. The Camry girl smiles. I hear Coke cans rolling under a car.

"Did they ask about bears?"

"No, they asked about TV."

My aunt and I laugh a little. This sort of conversation goes on while dinner heats up, with me wanting to know more about the most recent arrivals and my aunt wanting to watch more TV. A motel in the middle of nowhere is kind of a distracted family, and my aunt and my TV watching is pretty much an unchanging changing seasonal routine whenever I visit, eating and chatting slowly and occasionally as the night wears on, with the routine broken up only when the late night news comes on at three or four a.m. and my aunt shuffles in her Chinese slippers to the vending machines in the lobby where she buys some Ho Hos and puts them in a freezer for our dessert.

---

[1] How to Detect Lies—body language, reactions, speech patterns

The following techniques to telling if someone is lying are often used by police and security experts. ... The guilty person may speak more than natural, adding unnecessary details to convince ... Related Books: Never be Lied to Again ...

www.blifaloo.com/info/lies.php - Cached - Similar

What does it mean to "say" something about poetry? Or *in* poetry? What does it mean to say anything at all? We speak and then what? Judith Butler would tell us, after J.L. Austin, that words can act, can be injurious, like those times—we all know them—when you are walking down the street and the word ███████ is hurled heavy from a passing car window and the world stops, and the body falls out of itself, splits.

███████ ,

███████ ,

███████ ...

The word itself can be treated as gesture—the arm overhead cocked, hand cupped? Some of us want our poems to do this power work, to shrug or pout or flip off. What about the "artifacts of living" themselves? (Objects.) Are they not utterance in the most obvious sense, if being is speaking?

I'm inclined to think of utterance, in this time and place, as a kind of silence, or to borrow from John Cage, as traffic.

The challenge for the contemporary: how to speak into linguistic traffic? *So much has already been said. Bodies of harm.*

Here we are: pre-apocalyptic pulling together, a magnetizing, exponential multiplicity, language over language. She says one thing into my ear and simultaneously sends me a text. I'm reading her blog. Perhaps this is the height of the erotic.

Someone in a different context said, "His poems just move me so much." Barthes says, "I'm interested in language because it wounds or seduces me." There is a wetness in both wound and seduction (are they not the same thing?), I claim, an invitation to slip into the body, feel its irrational opening.

When I speak out loud—when I am talking—I am not thinking about speaking as much as I'm doing it, language, falling over from tongue to air, dissolving. But when I write I work to carve out something in between.

The in-between-ness in poetry interests me in that poetry can open what can seem like linguistic foreclosure—traffic, which is silence. Where language over language over object-utterance—the interstices of linguistic traffic—produces a shuddering. The desire here is to say something about poetry via adjacency, to produce in your body the internal gesture, and then a glimmering surface.

from THE MAIN CAUSE OF THE EXODUS

I, a dead woman. Hunt leaves as might a child. Swing up through my own lack, my own chaos. Hurt staged in the lung. They ask me of the paralytic, of the collapsed upper aperture.

But what of this human need, mouths my mute.

The I radiant in heat, polish. *I am closing my legs now.*

Subsiding against graffitied wall, pinched to hold up—

I must be a high fashion fucking model!

This negro type is ancient. The Egyptian monuments demonstrate its existence four thousand years ago. Unless the physiography of the landscape changes profoundly, the negro type will probably exist here four thousand years hence.

Land divides despite the shine of blackened skin, opens itself infinite, or a howl. [Too many bodies to count.]

Or how wonder works. When I am squatting to retrieve a cup of vaginal blood, and bearing down, as the instructions say, as in defecation, I am wondering.

Industrial children held—

Territory forgotten—

Territory bludgeoned—

—Why are all the children bound?

—They are all musicians.

Continual mouth breathing can affect the inner ear. Without good hearing the controlling factor of correct attack and good pronunciation is lost.

Their pleasant asylum—

And which contains?   Entertainments—

Shaken mumbled something   was—

supposed to be names—   Translated—

In whose service the pet—

—A kind white woman—in whose service—rescue—

It is wonderful the volume of sound that seemed to be hidden away in those small dusky bodies.

When the said they'd split me in two, I was overjoyed, wanting to get at the rip of things.

How to inhabit the sensation of living.

We are without allegiance. We are royal in our independence.

When the I speaks, it speaks into an other's speech. This is a labor. Next to her, a learned man is grey and wearing comfortable shoes. He does not think about the shoes, he simply wears them. He seeps. It's impossible to determine the monument of his instructional value.

They can't figure out why the rapes keep happening.

Blood point of needle. Carnal hovering. It is we who say, "they were protected" and at the same time "fetish."

[Yet,
fecund
pump]
pink-like
or
heavy
omission—
dare
to
god-dread
[body-panoramas]
blurred
constitution
[an avenue]

J. MICHAEL MARTINEZ

AISTHESIS: THE POETIC AS THE (I)-MMEMORIAL

Memory intimates double visions of the world: one sights an object, a scent inhaled—sensations call forth the unconscious' reservoir to surface like sediment stirred at river's bottom—one remembers. This is the common interpretation; however, rather than memory being dependent on these things (the scent of plum, orange's tart, the down of a lover's breath), could it be that these manifest are all dependent on remembrance for their fixity?

The taste, the shape, the very flavor of the plum or the lover's down is dependent not only on its sensual reality but is made total through memory's abstraction—knowledge of the object constitutes the object itself—and faith in past event is self-validated. This is to say: the memory of a thing is a belief in *memory* itself—the performance of memory makes "real" the fixity of memory's very conception—thus, I am content in faith with my own past.

If this, memory/history is not of the past, rather, it is the actual relation one has with the present: the art of remembrance is the living lens by which the phenomenal is made itself. This is not to say one is what one is not (subject and object as One); it is to say the phenomenal world chords and echoes as harmony with my unanchored mortality.

SELF-PORTRAIT AS THE POLAROID OF YOU

Many of the things
I desire are owed
to pictures:

this withdrawal of color into form,
kittens & creamer.

All the soft
preventing my own
absolute individual.

When I die, I want the young languages
to name the water
after you,

to paint on the pier
the vigor and goodness
of the devout,

to distinguish two points
between judgment
and perception:

our thoughts in what they represent,
& our head bound by the background.

SELF-PORTRAIT AS A GRIM TALE:
THE KING WHO TOOK HIS DAUGHTER TO THE BOILING

But before the daughter was the day an army of loyal servants wearing only silk slippers spread out in a hundred rows across a thousand acres of fauna. The animals fled these naked & their soft plodding. Poppies, wisteria, calla lilies were razed from earth & hung from pins onto sheets of vellum. The librarians organized the plants according to their alchemical properties—motherwort, lady's mantle, & mistletoe paged together under the heading of "Life Root." The books of fauna were taken to the cauldron's depth to the cauldron's culler. The albino culler opened the books of the flowers, dipped the thousand stems & petals, calyxes & bulbs into a molt of gold.

After the lily's fall & the wisteria's orbital ridges were shelled in amber, the King rushed from his throne with salivating hands. He took one of the culler's arrangements to his garden, planted it delicately in moist dirt. He climbed to his topmost tower. Purple robes fell over his crooked arms. He trumpeted orders from a conch shell. Wearing black cotton garments & leather boots, the servants spread out in obedience across the fields re-planting what had been torn.

But before the daughter & before the fauna was the day the King ordered three stones a day to be taken from his keep. Stone on stone for a thousand days of stone until all were pliable sublimations of light. White apron against albino face, the culler bowed. The king, seated on his throne, stood before his supplicants. He climbed to the highest mounds of golden blocks. Purple robes fell over his crooked arms. He trumpeted orders from a conch shell. Dressed in white cotton garments & barefoot, the servants, standing in one hundred & one rows, bowed simultaneously & set to the task of rebuilding. On the throne the king sat light-bowered, his frame a mineral embodied & alive.

SELF-PORTRAIT AS THE RECORD PLAYER'S NEEDLE

I carved a record out of frozen Irish creamer. I wanted it to sound like coffee poured through silk, a no-sound at the limits of reason. I sought to seduce you. But you wanted me to stop buying happiness: blue dog dolls, banker lamps, and puddles for birds. You wanted to run with me through worm-laden forests and shed black petals. But there is no movement between the object and my body, only these certainties: a match, a lamp, a self holding within its appearance.

SELF-PORTRAIT AS THE HINGE WITHIN THE FABLE

Imagine—in front of us—they silently pass. And they believe unrelated
      objects are organs
to recognize the human. And, again, we are no longer interruptions.

Imagine—in front of us—the beginning is not a study. And they believe
      the cicada's larva
reveals narrow secrets. And we accompany: to form, to shape.

Imagine—in front of us—a beautiful garden. And they believe color is
      the shoreline's end
where we abandon our too sudden bodies. And, here, we are carriers
      of different significance.

Imagine—in front of us—each word devolves a lexicon. And they believe
      shape shuts on a hinge
within the voice they fable. And, here, we slaughter the spring lambs.

Imagine—in front of us—they pass us between nature, between history.
      And they believe the door
alters the frame's flow. And we are a dark summer moving against oceans.

Imagine starlings circling in a postcard's blue. And they believe oration is
      the living thing, the end
of geometric space. And here, in full sunlight, we are gifts hoisted to the vanishing point.

SELF-PORTRAIT AS THE PERFUME OF THE WINTER WIND

Seasons ebb &, in its field, the bright harvesters of sands gather starved fragrance.

Inside, the house draws winter wind between the sun & the primeval net of work fine with the bloated leaves shedding our laughter.

In patience, the dark pasture fills with lambs & my tears shake out the space light sleeps by when spring is cold among the graves.

The hour turns, my shadow walks swanlike among the first birds moving the stars.

It would be a year or so before I would read Phillip Whalen's *Scenes of Life at the Capitol*, the poems of Joanne Kyger, or the travel dairies of Tu Fu or Basho. I think I had just read the notebooks of Gerard Manley Hopkins, which likely gave me the idea that I should notice processes, shifts of light or sounds rising and being subsumed by still other sounds. If I paid close enough attention for long enough, I thought, I could tune my senses to receive images and my poem could be a wax tablet onto which other forces would write.

I kept noticing the moths lost at floodlights in my apartment's parking lot and thought to make totems of them, to make some kind of projection into the moth's way of perceiving. Lepidopterists suggest that moths use the moon as a primary reference point and have the ability to calibrate their flight paths as the Earth's rotation causes the moon to move across the sky. Fresh out of graduate school I was scared and feeling alone, living in a tiny studio in Austin and hustling to make money and send some of it to my disabled mother who, back in California, was getting by on public assistance. I mention these circumstances because I never sat down to compose this particular poem so much as I committed to recording impressions as a way to hold on to the possibility of being a writer, even as my claim to that privilege was slipping. I liked very much the idea of turning off the floodlights and finding reference points that I hoped would let me navigate into the present moment and its layers.

Things rise and fall here; the train and cars weigh upon or sink into the earth even as the poem tries to move through personal and public darkness. And these seem to register in the poem by affect—a sense of simultaneous immersion in and alienation from the racial and economic histories and present circumstances of the struggling neighborhood where I lived and of the South more broadly. Moving by affect seemed a good way to avoid prescriptive statements or false lights. Not that these are bad, actually, but the older I get, the more I think we might get to say a thing or two before we die, but no more. In her lurching toward her own death, my mother said something I remember as, "Come back home now. When I die, you can go anywhere." That was too much, it made her too big a night, so I called her America and listened and kept writing.

DO THE MOTH

I.

      built for night
      twin quills in
      a single world
      of darker information

Today I saw a dropped bough
soften in the rising heat
of the road
blown open and closed
as the opposing cars made of it
a green-leafed

breathing bellows,
an after-life placed

down the yellow line of the median
to reveal the exchange
                happening like breathing
                    in which it lay.

In the cool dusk
my apartment's parking lot lets rise the cars
that sunk into its day.
I hear the paper music of pigeons
      in the alcove of the laundry and
           soon traffic will reclaim the passing horn
                of the train.

All poems are about money
           speak and incarnate themselves
in the plain language of money

and in reading
　　　poems I learn
I am buck stupid nothing

when I fall
　　　　　to the side of money
while in the main, money
　　　　　　　　　was there with its arms upturned.

The small tree in the city walk
pushes out a last array of fruit
before winter.

Is every southern city
the hopeful piling of stones
left over from Reconstruction?

　　　"The north　　is coming" —Canadians speaking of winter.

After the battle, the pockets will be gone through.
Eight months, my love tells me, to clear the bodies
　　　from Gettysburg.

Had my interior governors failed

I'd have said back, I'm sick　　　　I need an oil pressed
from the deepest brine in the ribs of fish,
in the imbricated muscles of fish.

Instead I say, I need to get some money or my mother will die.

All of this
while the sensate, open skin already exchanges with the minor
　　　　　gods, Love, the Messenger,

and all the small banners for sound—
motorcycle in the crotch,
pigeons, the paper bell cooing of pigeons.

II.

The train comes into the town
and the town stays upon the world
and the town stays upon the world.

Today my mother asked to be dead

and I look up from the floor of the supermarket struck by six people
who have come to this proximity and I come to believe
I should know their names.

What should a stranger do at your city's gates, your village's
outmost circle? What is the courtesy?

Nothing,
he just passes, we
are a free people.

He passes as the train pulls its pacer stack cars,
refrigerated tankers,
its gasses, and sloshing liquids through the town.

The parked sedans sink deeper into the street. The local pigeon flock picks
from the ant line outside my window,
the flock passes the noon ringing little bells inside their gullets I know

are made of moth wings, ATM receipts, and lantern paper.
The flock flocks, the flock sleeps, the flock nests in awning
alcoves above the RBM mart. Two public phones stand there.

Men come to them in fancy boots,
           to ring Mexico, Honduras
piss behind a dumpster between calls.

The dumpster stands in an industrial green the color of a planted
          forest; it sinks deeper.
             When I die, America says, you can go anywhere.

I try to know as little as possible when I'm writing poems. But it's a constant struggle, even for someone who, like me, doesn't know much (ha! doesn't know *anything*) to begin with. And the struggle isn't really with what one knows, or with what one will lazily allow oneself to believe one knows, but with one's awareness of what one knows. When writing, a poet shouldn't even know her own name. Composition, I think, is discovery; composition is capturing the moment of discovery and presenting it so that it registers as at least equal to the thing discovered. Even knowing how to tie a shoe can get in the way. Of course, it's pretty hard to forget one's own name, or how to tie a shoe (assuming one knows in the first place—it took me a long time to figure that last one out, and lately my double-knots haven't been working), so the best one can hope for is the suppression of one's awareness that one knows such things. I keep at it, though. My goal is to know a little less every day.

THE CARDINAL IS THE MARRIAGE BIRD

The cardinal is the marriage bird / And flies a flash of dusk

becomes   forgets becomes / Again the body

of the cardinal in the sunlight in the day   / Imagine

otherwise the cardinal in the room

The sunlight in the room in the day / The sunlight

on the snow the snow   like frosted glass   / The cardinal in the snow

as clear as if it were   on the inside side of the window

And not in the world the cardinal is

The marriage bird and flies   in the sunlight on the snow / Between the sunlight and the snow

a shadow on the snow but still / The sunlight on the snow

imagine otherwise

The cardinal on the windowsill

And flies

a flash of shadow and the cardinal is the shadow bird / A flash of wound   the wound

bird evergreen to evergreen

Wound leaping evergreen to evergreen / Imagine

welcoming the wound

MERCY

My first thought was   *My baby's sick* / Wasn't a thought

really but that's what all that blood / Felt like

but all that blood

Really but all that blood   felt like my Mary getting / Sick on my hand

Wasn't a thought my first thought   was I wasn't / Was   I hadn't but I couldn't stop

After the first

Cut I couldn't stop

because it hurt

I couldn't stop / Hurting her because it hurt   I had to cut her head / All the way off

The marshals came with the Master

I wasn't

Thinking about mercy or love

Before that night   I never had the chance to love   / Anyone

she was the first   person I loved

HOW TO RECOGNIZE IT

Master I learned from   more than anybody him

what love is how / To recognize it love

That's how I knew I was right to cut Mary's throat

Thinking of what he   did to me my

body what I knew he would

Do to Mary   to Priscilla cut   / Didn't just cut

and leave her body move

On to her sister   made   sure she was dead

I loved her   wanted her / Head to come off in my hands

WAS PRETTY WAS KIDS

Was pretty was kids

said I looked / Like Michael Jackson Michael Jackson 1982

And skinny sometimes   wouldn't eat for days

Was pretty and he saw it   was / Pretty he saw it too

Pretty for boys / To be a boy

Pretty it made him angry talked as if

It made him angry talked / Why

would I want to look like that / And didn't look at me   I thought

He didn't like me knew he

didn't like niggers and I was one   was half

Niggers and I was one   and wasn't also wasn't

old enough to be   afraid of him

the way a man   / Would

without love

he held me down face down

SHAME (MARY ARMSTRONG)

Old Polly Cleveland was   she was a Polly devil if

Ever there was one killed / My little sister just for crying tore

her diaper off

Whipped her to death was

nine months old when I was ten I got her back

Busted her eyeball with a rock

Belonged then to her daughter then

her daughter set me free   / In '63

And I went down to Texas found my mamma

It was still   slave time in Texas but I had my papers

when   / A white man put me on the block / I held my papers up

I wouldn't let him take them made him   stand to look   / I reck-

on any

white man there if we had been alone

He would've snatched those papers quick / I reckon it was

shame that saved me

so I don't never feel no shame

ANNA MOSCHOVAKIS

Sometimes people hold a core belief that is very strong. When they are presented with evidence that works against that belief, the new evidence cannot be accepted. It would create a feeling that is extremely uncomfortable, called cognitive dissonance. And because it is so important to protect the core belief, they will rationalize, ignore, and even deny anything that doesn't fit in with the core belief. ------- I'm not sure how to talk about what I've been writing recently. I can say that for me, the current debate between "the lyric" and "conceptual writing" is not a particularly useful one when framed as such, although many useful discussions have emerged from it. ------- My way of thinking is very particular and concrete. It doesn't follow a continuous path. ------- The aspect of that debate that turns on subjectivity is the most relevant, I think, to my recent poems. But I don't see any use in simply decrying the poetic assumption of an insoluble sovereign self, that persecuted lyric "I" that people love to hate. No poet I've ever stayed interested in has bought into that fiction, as far as I can tell (this could be due in part to the way I read). ------- So long as I have questions to which there are no answers, I will go on writing. ------- I am drawn to poems that appropriate language not because appropriation is a means to escape the expressivity reductively attributed only to lyricism (it's not) and not because, as a form of recycling or repurposing, it is somehow ethically superior to "original" writing—the compost heap of written linguistic content is so carelessly built, it may need the introduction of decontaminating mycelia more than it needs to be turned, again and again, to release its putrid smell—but because appropriation can contribute to a writing practice in which critique and affect collide, forming an irony that interests me now. ------- I try not to speak too much nonsense, or at least to speak only the nonsense I think. ------- If one of the tasks of writing is to model ways of being—including ones that appear to be out of reach, even to the writer, at the moment of writing—then this collision seems to me to provide a start. ------- But honestly, it's better to die on your feet than to live on your knees. ------- One in seven adults in the U.S. cannot read this sentence. ------- Any ground I might think I've found here is necessarily slick. ------- Whatever shoes you're wearing, you probably didn't make them yourself. ------- /fanon /antin /lispector /bosquet /zapata

WHAT IT MEANS TO BE AVANT GARDE

I feel sad.

I feel discouraged about the future.

I feel I have failed more than the average person.

As I look back on my life, all I can see is a lot of failures.

I don't get real satisfaction out of anything anymore.

I am dissatisfied or bored with everything.

I feel quite guilty most of the time.

I expect to be punished.

I am disgusted with myself.

I am critical of myself for my weaknesses or mistakes.

I blame myself for everything bad that happens.

I have thoughts of killing myself, but I would not carry them out.

I would like to kill myself.

I would kill myself if I had the chance.

I don't cry any more than usual.

I used to be able to cry, but now I can't cry even though I want to.

I am no more irritated by things than I ever was.

I am slightly more irritated now than usual.

I have lost all of my interest in other people.

I make decisions about as well as I ever could.

I can't make decisions at all anymore.

I am worried that I am looking old or unattractive.

I feel there are permanent changes in my appearance that make me look unattractive.

I have to push myself very hard to do anything.

I don't sleep as well as I used to.

I wake up several hours earlier than I used to and cannot get back to sleep.

I get tired from doing almost anything.

My appetite is not as good as it used to be.

My appetite is much worse now.

I have lost more than five pounds.

I have lost more than fifteen pounds.

I am worried about physical problems like aches, pains, upset stomach, or constipation.

I am very worried about physical problems and it's hard to think of much else.

I have not noticed any recent change in my interest in sex.

I have lost interest in sex completely.

I was in the park when they called   with my head on my knee and my nose in a book
the book was by david antin, an american   there are many ways to follow a thought
when the phone rang they told me they wanted me   there was a voice on the phone that
belonged to a man   it sounded like a man and him saying they wanted me   I read a book
the other day by a circus performer   in my youth I read a book by an anthropologist's
son   who ran off with the gypsies with his parents' blessing   he was not an american
american parents don't say yes   you can run off with the gypsies because it might be
interesting   the circus performer was unstable emotionally   she committed suicide at
the age of forty-two   the man said we want you to come in for some tests   the parents
hoped the boy would grow up to write a book   in which he would detail the functioning
of roma culture   before the phone rang I was reading the bit in the antin   about how
it's a really good thing to be on the fringe   the roma lie to everyone except to their own
coterie makes you soft   when I went in for the tests they said I was normal   and only
after I did a lot of research on the internet   did I come to understand what they meant
by that   was that my condition is unexplained

I feel downhearted and blue Most of the time.

Morning is when I feel the best Some of the time.

I have crying spells or feel like it Good part of the time.

I have trouble sleeping at night A little of the time.

I eat as much as I used to Good part of the time.

I still enjoy sex A little of the time.

I notice that I am losing weight Some of the time.

I have trouble with constipation [   ]

My heart beats faster than usual A little of the time.

I get tired for no reason Good part of the time.

My mind is as clear as it used to be A little of the time.

I find it easy to do the things I used to Some of the time.

I am restless and can't keep still Most of the time.

I feel hopeful about the future A little of the time.

I am more irritable than usual Most of the time.

I find it easy to make decisions [   ]

I feel that I am useful and needed Some of the time.

My life is pretty full A little of the time.

I feel that others would be better off if I were dead Most of the time.

I still enjoy the things I used to do [   ]

I had forgotten the name of the boy who ran with the gypsies   it was mid-morning and I was sitting at my desk   taking the last sip of my morning decaf with soy   the last sip is always cold and unsatisfying   this was not my first attempt to recover the boy's name   I had of course forgotten the title of the book as well   I typed dutch gypsy narrative young anthropologist into my machine   for fifteen years I have been trying to recall the name of the boy or of the book   I may even have unsuccessfully searched for it before   during those years I recreated a memory of the narrative   he is beloved by the group and accepted as one of them   he does not miss his parents though he holds them in high esteem   he learns to sing from a thin dark man and to steal from a thin dark girl   the boy himself is as blond as a broom   the feeling of not-knowing is like flying in your dreams   around the time I started searching I stopped dreaming anything fun   dutch gypsy narrative young anthropologist did the trick   the name came up and I remembered it   recognition makes you fall but you can try to resist   though you'll make yourself ridiculous flapping all around   I switched windows and searched for my unexplained condition   there are lots of others who have it and none of them can spell   I was wrong about the search being successful   the name I thought I recognized was of a different person   an 18th-century abolitionist who fell in love with a slave   he slept with many of them but only fell in love once   I did another search and this time left out nationality   I typed son of anthropologists runs off with gyspies   when mysteries are explained they don't exactly disappear   the boy was belgian not dutch and that had been my mistake   the flemish part of belgium not the part where they speak french   the man called back to say one of my test results had been compromised   the title of the book is *the gypsies*

Feeling nervous, anxious or on edge Nearly every day.

Not being able to stop or control worrying More than half the days.

Worrying too much about different things Several days.

Trouble relaxing More than half the days.

Being so restless that it's hard to sit still Several days.

Becoming easily annoyed or irritable Nearly every day.

Feeling afraid, as if something awful might

POETICS (OF BLACKNESS)

1.

Poetry is rhythm breaking something to say that broke rhythm, an afterlife installation where knowledge takes the form of pauses, a soundscape made of risen questions, a machine made out of what happened when we were together in the open in secret. It miscommunicates catastrophe with unseemly festivity, in an obscenity of objection; it knows not seems, it doesn't know like that, its Julianic showings go past meaning, in social encryption, presuming the form of life whose submergence it represents. But it doesn't represent. It more and less than represents. There's a rough, unsutured transaction that moves against repair to make a scar. Poetry is a scar. It's hard to look at something when you can't look away.

2.

The social life of poetry strains against a grammar that seeks to defy both decay and generativity in the name of a self-possessed equivalence that, in any case, you know you can't have because you know you can't have a case. Some folks strive for that impossibility, rather than claim the exhaustion they are and have, as if this were either the only world or the real one. Encrypted celebration of the ongoing encryption is an analytic of the surreal world in and out of this one. It's not about cultural identity and it's not about origin; it's the disruptive innovation of one and the voluntary evasion of the other.

3.

The commitment to repair is how a refusal to represent terror redoubles the logic of representation. The refusal of our ongoing afterlife can only ever replicate a worn-out grammar. The event remains, in the depths. The event-remains are deep and we stand before them, to express them, as their expression. These bits are a mystery, a new machine for the incalculable, which is next, having defied its starting place. I almost remembered this in a dream, where we were just talking, and nothing happened, and then it was over, until just now, with your hands, and light on the breeze's edge. I just can't help feeling that this is what we're supposed to do—to conserve what we are and what we can do by expansion, whose prompt, more often than not, shows up as loss (which shows up, more often than not, as a prompt). More shows up more often than nought if you can stand it.

EVE IS A TEXTURE DAVE IS CENTERING.

eve is a texture
dave is centering
our whirring be
your bird ok
in government
and binding
nothingness is
in capacity
a moisture
unsurrounds
our gathering
and pouring
our came and
sent our drop
of chocolate of
a song in hand
our open bowl in
studio in assyrian
air in oil in serenade
interrogate our leaves
and air in saying
savoring of air
in stir from talk
of searing and
enhanced to hand
our salad is your
touch extreme
and braided fingers
dressed in sugar
through emulsion
like a spur your
final plural curve

AJ, THIS IS FOR UNDERNEATH YOUR BEAUTIFUL PROOF
OF CONCEPT.

Man, it is but it ain't

                    fold or fold in or lay out or spin or walk away array

arrange. free

keep fading   aanic tape and flash and shit and

broken stream

I thought was streamed with rhythm where we went awry

        are we a broken category

                                 lull between

pings but no hard inside pulse and more than open enough to not get bothered or to
stand being bothered by overlap or by somebody watching or by somebody else but if it is
somebody else or if he is here this could be her sound.

I LAY WITH FRANCIS IN THE MARGIN.

I lay with francis in the margin.
my plan without surrounding
was in tact. my shift was extra
vagrant. my grain was terrible

and in decision was immigrant
and trans, I'm just so sensitive
and flighty, but francis curls me
into violet cradling and reading

to prepare for bordering and a
foundation for numbering into
violent edging. francis, who's so
careful in the sight of his mama,

in her recital of handing, in her
unsold morsels, keeps straight
to the ornament's advance, man.
his lists are like knives and his

tongues, oh my god, are sweet as
maths. we're like westerns in a
togetherness; viv richards is our
accident and unforeseen exam.

RA, THIS ECHO OF YOUR GIGNITY

over
heard
in pitts
burgh
4.5.13

but it turns out that everybody be returning our calls.
we were talking at easter dinner, in a thai restaurant,
about our favorite coefficients. never found a solution
talking about the problem, abandoned to ourselves in
piracy, enemies to all our states and selves; but from the
moment we get traction to the moment we lose track
we study sharing like players study playing. playing just
to play transfections of repertoire as strategies and tactics
of sharing to the end of the world. can we share the end
of settling? can I misunderstand you again, man, out of
love for extra? the north star is what's happening now
so I'm listening to difference in the joy of being extra,
which is the problem of the centuries. listening in pan-
african pan, resorbed in all for you, original suffer head,
like a new series of famous flames on bridge street, this
gspianic sound and ex cathedran groove is the original.

GRAD GRIND, GENTLES, TILL THE PARK IS GONE.

his hair was like furry lining brushed and see-through and he was pale, his pinkness had a descent in it, like he had warmed down,

but you could tell by the way he took up space, scared somebody would get him for all that careless bumping into people,

trained in expansion at an early age, his demands at the informational meeting were sharp and unchecked in his mother's

dead arms, with her metal hands,

and his father explained the proper use of the materials to the principal. maria and cesare and the theory of handcuffs,

asking for what they took because it's hot as hell between the baguette, don't bring your own tamales, and the house of york.

the plan when we were surfing was to blow that school up with some extra words, urge kilombo more than across, get us some land.

look at durham in my window.

SAWAKO NAKAYASU

FROM "INFREQUENTLY ASKED QUESTIONS"

Q: What is a poem?

A: A long time ago when Josh first asked me to write something for EWC [Evening Will Come] I wrote this down:

"I'm growing a bit more straightforward with age, for whatever that's worth. (By 'age,' I simply mean that I am twice as old as my students, which seems to be a marker of some sorts.) Anyway, after being invited to write a poetics statement, I've been tossing the idea around in my head. I can't remember the last time anyone ever asked me to write a poetics statement, and in fact the last time might have been my first time, which was at the end of my very first poetry workshop (when I was 18, the same age as my current students). I believe we were asked to write poetic manifestos, and I can embarrassingly remember writing something about words reaching out of the page to grab your balls. (That's also around the age I discovered sex and that's probably all I had on my mind at the time.) So the last time I had put any thought to this, maybe a couple of days ago, I was vaguely recalling a long-ago lecture given by the ever brilliant, ever abstruse Kenjiro Okazaki at the Yotsuya Art Studium, facing a photocopied handout with a Kant excerpt, impossibly translated into Japanese, somehow concluding that somewhere in there, Kant had proclaimed that poetry was the source of all art. So just now I was on the brink of posting this on my Facebook status: 'Is there anyone out there who can explain to me the part in Kant where he says that poetry is the source of all art?' But I chose not to, as I do with many potential Facebook status updates that go unposted. I could have looked it up for myself, obviously, and sort of gestured at that, but then I decided it wasn't really my thing to be quoting Kant anyway. I'll say it in my 'own' words: poetry is the source of all art."

September 2011

FROM "CLOSE ENOUGH TO EACH OTHER FOR THE EAR TO BE AFFECTED"

Poetry. Poetry reading. Poetry slam. Poetry therapy. Poiēsis. Point of view of Polish political verse. Politics and poetry. Polynesian poetry. And polysemy, and polysyndeton, and Portuguese poetry, and postcolonial poetics and postmodernism. And post-structuralism. Poulter's measure replaced by pentameter. Prakrit poetry. Prague school or Parisian préciosité, pursuit of politesse and purity. Present a pre-romantic pregunta to the Pre-Raphaelite Brotherhood, later promulgated by Pre-Raphaelitism. Power of the present, priamel or prelude.

August 2013

4.6.2004

Texture of a field of fried umbrellas.

They are arranged so neatly that one wonders if there are small children beneath them, holding hands so as to keep the rows intact and the columns true, in spite of whatever kind of weather may come. Enough fresh oil was used in the frying of these umbrellas that theoretically they should repel any sort of fluid which takes a shot at the field, and in fact this is true, but the unfortunate inherent shape of umbrellas encourages the rain to slip inside the crevices between one fried umbrella and another, getting the toes of the children wet, whether they are there or not.

6.10.2003

Some take issue with eating the eyeballs of fish. Small fish, I can eat them easily, with pleasure, eyeballs and all. Their eyes are small enough that they look drawn in, a dot from a pencil. Women and their brows, sometimes I catch a woman with an overzealous pencil, drawing an expression of surprise right onto her own face. All day, water-resistant.

In London, Bruce Nauman stabs himself in the eye with his finger again. And again.

In a painstakingly fancy restaurant in Tokyo, the last dish to arrive is not a fish, but a fish head. Resistance player. We take it apart, joyfully carrying the white meat to our mouths, but all I remember is after we had turned the poor fish inside out and around to get at all the meat, accidentally wandering towards its eyeball, big and juicy and dead. I didn't mean to poke, really I didn't. Didn't eat it, really we couldn't.

I wake up with a shoulder in my eye. A constant, a sleeping shoulder like a rock, and I push my eyeball into the shoulder, then out, then the other eye. Cried all day yesterday and the pressure is good, a relief, to be held against the solid and round and sleeping surface. The kindness of stillness. Moments of pressure.

My eye always stops giving at a certain point, as much shoulder as I can take at any given moment.

11.16.2003

The pain of seeing something beautiful.

Is layered as such, the first layer of it being thick, of substance, I can't say which sort, but of being matter and matterful, or rather, a person for whom I have spent a great deal of time and love, and this layer would be this very time and love, in whatever physical form it may take shape.

Then there are many layers of something else, everything else, the world, for example, or more likely simply a space of time or geography or perhaps a curtain or a collared shirt or a person or several, various degrees of people and objects.

The last layer is the something beautiful, which lays itself down quietly on top of all these layers, none of which were waiting for this to happen, except that only by the happenstance of the arrival of this layer are the other layers actualized as such; a distance, a thickness, a slightly twitching texture is created between the first and last layers, a measurable distance that surfaces out of nowhere but an internal and external longing for a presence or good word.

9.19.2004

for Nada and Gary

Whenever I meet new people I want to touch them first and find out their texture.

I also do this in stores when I am shopping, so shopkeepers hate me. I turn to the person on my left and ask very gently if I can lick his or her eyeball. The food arrives and I place a slice of raw cow tongue in my mouth, because someone once told me that this is absolutely the sexiest food item in the world. Do you like kissing cows.

I get up to go to the restroom, but the person on my right, instead of moving out of the way, offers to me his or her arm, with a large gash from last week's motorcycle accident. There is an awkward moment, and then I sit back down so that I am more stable. I clean off my right hand before I touch, ease my finger inside and then further, some asshole at the other end of the table is making stupid sound effects, but in any case I am soon unaware of everything oh no everything at all, and if I were not myself at this moment I would probably have to avert my eyes, unable to watch as a certain virginity is lost, and then lost.

9.24.2003

A standard commercial airplane flying a standard trans-Atlantic or Pacific route with the standard set of economy, business, and first-class passengers and correspondingly standard crew of pilots, flight attendants, and in-flight meteorologists.

This very aircraft also filled to the brim and every cranny with diamonds, and the flight attendant who wades her way slowly, patiently, through the stones and down the narrow aisle, pushing the usual cart of drinks, peanuts, Salisbury steak and long-ago fried potatoes, and what her face looks like at the end of it, and just then the diamond that drops out from under the neath of her skirt.

I was first trained in the style of Louise Glück, my earliest teacher, and still one of the poets whose possible remarks I hear in my head when I write. Glück taught me the value of what she called intelligence in poetic writing. She taught me to prize being nimble. But after my first education at Williams College, and Warren Wilson College's MFA, a series of adventures in reading led me to other quarters, first to the ecstatic lyric of Hart Crane, then to the coterie lightness of the New York School, then—once I moved west—to the combinatory sentences of the Language Poets. These adventures also led me back and forth across the boundaries between poetry in the university, and poetry as an urban subculture.

When I look at my poems, then, I see early confessional first-person accounts of being queer (mostly unpublished poems from my early twenties), compress into dithyrambs as I start to wonder what lies beyond coming-of-age frameworks. Later, around the time of my first book, I see experiments with short stanza forms, couplets and triplets, whose aim I only later realized was to figure out what interval of disjunction would suit me, since I always wanted to write poems that featured a speaker capable of such disjunction, rather than a poetry that used disjunction to critique the institution of the speaker. Those stanza forms, and the local weather they create, still interest me. Recently, though, I've become interested in what they can do if they are nested, so to speak, in different rhetorical registers. I'm interested in poems within poems. And I like the moments when a poem signals that poetry is present somewhere nearby, or offstage. I don't see this as "postmodern" or even meta-discursive in some capital-T theoretical way; or as "tradition," quite. I think of it as a rough equivalent to the moments in popular songs when the singer mentions hearing a song, or references singing, or sings about the DJ. I enjoy each poem's participation in the category "poetry" as a buoy and a stay.

Just a quick thought about tone. I know I get read as "ironic," and I know that's fair. But for me the force of irony is greatest, not when it bespeaks cleverness about the state of the world, but bafflement and dismay and indiscreet hope. I'm always thinking of my place in a three-generation immigrant narrative that starts working-class, becomes suburban, and ends up, with me, academic— and thinking about how I can never be sure which lines, which turns of phrase, would leave those earlier generations blank, or make them marvel, or disappoint them. I worry about being a smarty-pants. I'm the beneficiary of a lot of expensive education, and I fear that it may have deformed my sense of what intelligence is, including poetic intelligence. I fear that our best working definitions of being smart are possessive, or worse, entrepreneurial. So a lot of the movement of my poems involves trying to maintain a sense that intelligence is or should be a cousin activity to companionability, even solidarity; to physical grace. I have high hopes. But maybe only anthology readers can judge ...

THREE CINNABAR FIELDS

What if I said, I will supply the gear
I will offer you this seashore
I will give these birds a certain puckish idea of career

Write a poem called Flag
Write a poem that starts I flag beneath the tide of where the energy is up there in
    the trees

I will supply the brain
I will give you a jelly in which phrases are caught

Maybe you're thinking let it not be said of me, he wanted so much
Let it not be said, he spent all that energy trying to have a sensation again

But what if I said, I will give you that feeling
I will give you whatever the plural of plexus is

You know I'd like 'plexus' to be Greek since sitting here swooped over by gulls I feel so
    Orthodox
I feel bejeweled
I feel as though my attention would remain courteous and undisruptive should any lyric
    wind blow by

This is better and less manic than how I usually feel
Imagine a slicer-and-dicer you could use to get certain Indigo Girls songs to say things
    like 'there's not enough world in this room for my pain'
I mean god bless the Indigo Girls

So I am closer than before
Closer to my god
Closer to knowing the difference between an icon indicating a button nearby and an
    icon that is the button

I love 'my' intransitively, as in 'oh my'

I love the wonderful demotic Kantianism of everyone walking around these days
      expressing doubt by saying 'as *if*'

I love the recombinant banal, the 'nan' in it like ananda

Someone down the beach is playing 'Cascades of Color'
The surfer picks up his board and goes

AS IF TO SAY

So I'm digging these new forms of compositional helplessness

"I bring to this project an immense wind"

I try to write descriptively,

But it all comes out a calligram: check-mark inanition: flicked wrist of creation

the gaming movement of the vowel sounds
chorus and apostrophe

Only your prettiness is keeping you free

not the Olivetti storm-cloud of the first half-century
not the halo or the movement of the hand

Still between the perspectival foreground and the nauseating chaomorphosis beyond the
       garden wall I manage to imagine the city as a series of instructable   sparks

As if freaked with sociability
As if to say the topmost layer of the misery comes off and we can love again

       not Thom but the eddies of his having been here

first-person usurpations of indifferent pentameter
the psychic and the topical

I seriously have a mind of winter
But you: San Francisco: lightest pressure of a snowshoe on the carpet of pollen:
       someone singing Shambala

Divide your Palladian year by ten, how much does that mean a month is?

I don't know   it was spring

DOLORES

This one time? We went out into the street

The horns impressed us with the emptiness of every defiant gesture, and the drums
    suggested a permanent delay

But we went into the street, in goliardic mischief and eternal joy

Night fell; day broke
I want to write we felt like [   ]-ists but even partial words are searchable now so let's
    just say a band of outsiders

Politics had been given the name of a woman and I was fine with that

I thought, if I have children, will they still feel like this in 2046?
I thought, does having been a soixante-huitard make you young and beautiful until the
    day you die?

Fog rolled in and formed unstable patterns of reference
Lyrics floated by

And if disport could yield in fools simplicity completely unlike foolishness, we felt like
    that

    Simple like the hymns that greet creation

Bonjour! we said to the police —

Hi, this is the riot act? Hi.

CARESSED

The body is amazing

You could just decide, I want really strong *ankles*

Various plastic and rubber devices can be used to train it

A movement of the limbs can say, this is how much space there is in business for charisma

Leather Nikes in the '90s, signifying triumph over technical obstacles

"It also has that wet look"

Depending on your nationality, your body can be "packed in ice and wrapped in cellophane"

Depending on the signal I may or may not be able to find it

Packed dance floors in slow motion / everybody on their cell

The body "has been announced so many times that it cannot occur"

But it comes to life in carnival situations
It is capable of feelings incommensurate with personhood

From the pagan version it has gone from being sculpture to being vector, but for what

Dashed hopes in the little Parthenon
Karaoke glory and "a touch of the gai savoir"

When the body goes limp so limps the world

Soft as the slug's antenna

Though my hair turn white I will not harden against it

When I was very small, four or five, growing up in the D.C. area, I had access to a reel-to-reel song player; this was brought from Saigon by my parents. I could listen to reels of Vietnamese folk songs and also the "greatest hits" of Johnny Cash. I think the image of me, a child of Vietnamese/Euro-American descent, is captured in that musical range, in between two different kinds of folk song. Sometimes I think of my poems as a kind of spoken/sung folk song, a bit punky and dissonant, but still a folk song. I'm interested in naming, the sonic features of language, and making poems that hover in the sounding place between speech and music.

As a very young girl, I learned Vietnamese, a tonal language, but lost it entirely through the rupture of radical displacement. It was the experience of amputation, not unlike the orphan that words are, displaced in the moment of being born, immediately orphaned from its parent-object. I think of language as always being that—a reaching after—and often I think I write poems toward a lost language and a lost referent. That I might be trying, through poetry, to create and excavate some shape of a ghostly imprint.

When I approach writing, I ask how the maker of the poem and the poem itself can create a context to speak to a larger public circumstance. I like to think of poems as having many contours and textures: the internal and the external, the historical and the personal, the ordinary and the profound. I want poems that feel alive and that enliven, so that they become a kind of environment to enter.

HOA NGUYEN

UP NURSING

Up nursing   then make tea
The word war is far

      "Furry" say my boy
about the cat

I think anthrax
     and small pox vax

Pour hot water on dried nettles
Filter more water for the kettle

Why try
to revive the lyric

WRITE FUCKED UP POEMS

Write fucked up poems   round or layered
You know   cabbaged and I will egg you
Full moon   Spring Equinox
just passed and heavy rose blooms
unseasonably cold   and record snow

The rose is called "Katy Road"

A fucked poem from the start and the
rattling beak of Road Runner
in the driveway   descending cry
of Road Runner
eater of snakes and lizards

Egg in the sky   May
a fertile time
Strawberries from CA

In the Magic Kingdom
lies Tomorrow Land
the "first great malls" and
the "worship of vehicles"

Tape a stone over your womb
named *Black Apache Tears*

A DEBT

"A debt or credit bubble"
House as weight or anchor
Pop it open like champagne
Party like that year
You can pour nostalgia
Make a depreciation
Lovely or lonely
There is no time
to slow down!
Today's word: homeless
Homeless: home-less "without
a place to live"

WE MIGHT BE FOLDING

We might be folding laundry   I am fucked
having never learned to start a fire without matches
Now I'm boy scouted   I'm cooking eggs
Are grackle eggs edible

Stringy meat from scavengers surely

We could eat "Turks' Cap" pods or
insects   (rollie pollies?)
but there aren't enough of them either and likewise
he realizes my bee-keeping dreams are gauzy
with no uncomfortable moments
like Little House on the Prairie
          the televised one   with freckles

Walk from the taco shop
with fat styrofoam boxes

I'm almost as old as Old Elvis
          without the pain pills

Should really collect shoes
of future sizes for our boys' feet

My oven says clear/off
My toilet seats are new
& "Made in China"

For lunch
What did I have for lunch

The boys are monitored in front

of electronics

so I could have poetry and cook

First it was too warm
and now very cold with icy threats and
The National Guard in Missouri

How Polar Bears are melting in the drowning spaces

There is no room in the shiny expensive car
to take us all to California

PUSA

Old English   *pusa*   "bag"
Something soft and cuddly

What a beautiful pussy you are you are you are

"Love the world   stay inside it"

My own private pussy   and the feminist claims I make
that I pour a glass of wine for
and cultivate   growing a child

2 parabolic jaws
to eat fruit-flavored gummy teeth   Dracula style

Of Mona Lisa's smile
emotion recognition programs determine
83% happy   9% disgusted   6% fearful   2% angry

I wrote most of the poems from the "Animus" section of *Black Peculiar* in a very short period of time—very much stream of consciousness. I was on a plane on my way to the Squaw Valley Writers Workshop in 2009, got into a zone with the "Mostly to uncover the reality of…" pieces, and just kept going for the ten days I was there. I wrote about three dozen poems in the span of those ten days, but ended up including only about half of them in the book. A few months later, during research as I was putting the book together, I came across Jung's theories on the animus. I latched quickly onto it as the mode I had entered with those poems. I felt the "he" voice so strongly that I knew there had to be something more behind it than just a poetic conceit. The stories in my head from women I knew, from what I have witnessed, and from women whose stories I read about seemed to share a common thread of male violence and subjugation of their voices, so much so that those male voices became the ones repeated in our heads instead of our own, continuing an often destructive patriarchal narrative. During revision I tried many different forms for the poems—making them fragmentary, creating line breaks, playing with formal elements. But even though generally I find that breaking the sequential qualities of language and centering it in the body often undermines patriarchal accents, with this section the voice (already deeply centered in the body) needed no interruptions or intermediaries. The voice itself was the disruption, drawing attention to both the meaning under the words and of the words simultaneously, with allegorical qualities that made the work a natural fit for the prose form.

MOSTLY TO UNCOVER THE REALITY OF
MY DESTRUCTIVE HUNGER

He gave me nothing to eat but photographs of other people eating meat. Cooked and raw, half-gone and about to be sliced. In the photographs the people looked relaxed and not very hungry. But first they were killing the animals with their careful machines. This was before clumsy hands came to the collective mauling. And before the children danced carefully in their ironed clothes at their little table. It all looked delicious. The shiny weapons and thick spats of flesh and slavering mouths and families. He did this in order. In order that I might see how feeding is done.

MOSTLY TO UNCOVER THE REALITY OF
MY SOOTHING BRAND OF SICKNESS

I called a dangerous man my husband and something inside me loved it, loved the way each day he killed me a little more, killed himself a little more. There were ways of believing everything he said. Sometimes it meant folding my thoughts into tight squares with sharp edges that nicked my tongue as I held them underneath. Sometimes it meant hiding parts of myself in pissy alleyways and abandoned parking lots where they got slept on and rained on, pushed around in shopping carts or made a doorway on some tired body's flimsy house, so that I ended up a vagina with half a heart and no deep breaths. He never wanted or missed me but he wanted to, his brutal attachment burning the inside of me like an etching, toxic and harsh in its carefully planned beauty. I almost believed I could take it. One day I thought I couldn't fight anymore and then a sudden shift: I hustled a latticework of craving between blows. I unlocked my chorus of archetypal women from their chains. They rubbed their raw wrists with aloe and set to work.

MOSTLY TO UNCOVER THE REALITY OF
MY FREAKISH DESIRE TO PLEASE

He contorted my body, my emotions, my tongue into the bloom of a silk tree, making the buds trace the broken plates of his lips, tasting after origins, information, black holes. He says I am given over to convulsive pretending, that I toss and turn all night counting the times I was wrong and saying sorry. Sorry out loud to him, his body lying next to mine, muscular with greed and soft hands as a kind of mercy. At first he was all sympathy and charm, smelled of sandalwood and smoke, fingering the back of my neck and I was easy, crossed my ankles at the small of his back, *just this one last time.*

MOSTLY TO UNCOVER THE REALITY OF
MY IMPERATIVE NEED TO TRULY UNDERSTAND
THE NATURE OF ALL ANIMAL BEHAVIOR

He told me a story. In the story, one dog snarls at another. The snarling, scruffy dog has one blue eye, one brown eye and a chewed off tail. It is lean and its tongue is muddy—it licks dirt. It eyeballs and stalks the other dog, hanging that tongue over the other dog's head. The other dog leans into the pant: it's a small dog, fluffy and well loved. Before opening his mouth to the fluffy dog's head, the scruffy dog goes completely silent. The fluffy dog licks the muddy tongue. A pale man in a black suit leans toward the scruffy dog, points at the fluffy one, says, "Go ahead, boy. Go on. Get your snack."

MOSTLY TO UNCOVER THE REALITY OF
MY ULTRAINTERIOR CRUELTY

I refuse all medical treatment especially when going into labor so he shushes the surfacing alarm with a crisp whipcrack and I bite into the animal article my right hand nodding at the punishment coveting blinders and nosebleeds pressing my open face into a sterile pillow defiant in the name of contamination. *I appreciate your café au lait delusions* he says with a loud snort and tossing out 7 mimes and a daft intruder I couldn't bear to cuff. *Spinnbarkeit!* he said magic words flushing 1,000,001 clandestine hours of hiding preserved in shorthand down a bitter sinkhole—small waves swishing. *There is a loophole* he says. *You can obsess about rattraps and obscure public incidents.* Later an ob-gyn snapped the balance with neat-cut contrition. You can speculate.

ANDREA REXILIUS

My work investigates the book as a process of inquiry and is interested in the nature of conversation, questioning, subjectivity, women's history, and the proximity between physical self and textual self. In my writing and teaching I combine interdisciplinary research with creative process to spawn an approach that is both rigorously intellectual, in the sense of questioning, critical thinking, and essaying, as well as playful and engaged across the disciplines of performance, film, and installation. Related research interests include: contemplative performance poetics, book arts, text-off-the-page, feminism, and aesthetic theory.

My most recent book, *Half of What They Carried Flew Away*, is based on two major concerns. The first was to ask how one writes from both a narrative and anti-narrative structure simultaneously. How can one sustain a longer duration in writing without relying on narrative techniques like plot, character, or climax? What else might sustain and propel a narrative? The answer of this book was related to the idea of "residences." These residences (in the book named: desire, water, emanation, weather, and territory) speak to the different ways language inhabits space or how people inhabit language. These habitations might be intimate, ghosted, alien, contradictory, etc.

The second concern of *Half of What They Carried Flew Away* was around pronouns and how one might allow a multi-vocal narrator or lyric speaker to speak intimately regardless of that voice's distance from one specific physical body. So for example, how a speaker referred to as "they" might more accurately be speaking as an "I." And in turn, considering how the typical lyric speaker "I" might be heard as a less personal, and more porous consciousness. This text attempts to dispossess "they" and "I" from themselves and hopes to allow us to hear anew how these pronouns, minus their referents, inhabit a text.

As far as my writing practice goes, I don't write every day. Sometimes I don't write for months. What typically happens is I feel a silence, or maybe attention is a better word. I don't write for months, but I feel something going on at the back of the silence/attention. I read and notice and probably begin to curate some ideas, build some questions, but I don't know them and then one day I just do, and that's when I begin writing again. So maybe that is to say that the idea or the question comes from a level of consciousness that is not immediately accessible via language. I wait for it to become accessible and in the meantime I try to nourish it.

Final paragraph excerpted from a 2011 Bookslut interview by Olivia Cronk

WHAT IS THE EMANATION OF THEIR IMAGE?

They are from the early 1870s.
They move from house to house like windows.
They rise and fall.
They are a demonstration.
They continue to drift.
Some become informants.
They represent an emergence.
They are marginal. They move in rivulets.
They exist not only in their details.
They contain their own extraordinary destiny.
They live beside a family of small farmers.
They are discovered and decide to emigrate.
Their name is William.
They are born a little girl.

*

I do not know what it is they are like. What they move through feels like water. It is difficult for them to distinguish what is above from what is below. Clods of earth become not just synonymous, but identical to clouds. They often weep in the driest of climates. Moments recede from them. It is difficult for them to see what they are looking at. They are very close and very far from objects. When they speak one cannot locate the exact position of their mouths. Often they are recognizable in fields, though not readily apparent, one can sense them in the absences.

In the twenty-first iteration, they were disappointed their bodies were made of celluloid. After a while, they came to inhabit animals, trees, spots of light in the sky.

In the 1950s, they operated by a series of inversions, turning song into spirit. They sang and this singing flew into kinetic movement. It was noted. Singing belongs to the taxonomy of ascension. All things the voice catches on: air, clouds, vapor, smoke, foam, steam. To make manifest a reply. The flickering energy of the pulse as music. It looks out invitingly, where there are no boundaries. Not even between their sexes.

THIS IS THE ANSWER OF THEIR FOURTH CROSSING.

I am a common principle.

I have lived upon this earth.

I seek peace and solace.

I place a hundred dead bees on the windmills.

I am waiting for you to notice my boundary.

I have hoped to photograph each physical state.

I am my own reflection in the water.

I am doubling back to impend.

I am living in the land of water.

With all my power I behold my face.

The motif of appearance is deeper than recognizing an exterior.

I inhabit and experience it.

It is a state akin to revelation.

I am seeing myself as a mother, as if seen by someone else.

It is dizzying to have these eyes.

*

I've never slaughtered a pig. I've never actually seen an actual pig get slaughtered and I've never seen anyone actually die in front of me. I've never killed anybody on purpose and then watched them die in front of me. Nobody, it seems, has ever tried to kill me. There have been three exact moments so far in my life I've thought I was really going to die, and once I even resigned myself to death, but I didn't die. I eat animals. I've never given birth to any other person. My tragedies have all redeemed themselves as gifts. I am naïve. An hour into *Jaws*, after a teenage girl and a young boy have been gruesomely devoured and dismembered by the shark, hundreds of families still gather at the beach to celebrate Independence Day together, but no one dares go into the water, yet everyone, especially the mayor, wants to believe the shark isn't actually a problem. Finally, after some goading, one family of five is encouraged to be the first to enter—three happy kids floating on an inflatable raft, splashing and laughing, flanked by their mother and father with twisted grieving faces. This is what it feels like to write a poem for someone as naïve as me, the lowering of my sugary body into the bloody feeding pools. They are naïve too, this family, foolish even—they are offering their legs up to the shark in the false name of play—a seduction of grief. In Godard's *Vivre Sa Vie*, when Nana is transfixed in the dark theater by the grief in Joan of Arc's face, she knows something new of her own pain. She lowers herself into the sea of it, like an offering. And also, in Enrique Martinez Celaya's painting *Untitled (Boy)*, there is a yellow dot the size of a quarter on the pinkish bird-shaped heart of a boy I've stared at so much that it is now inside me, on my own bird heart. A yellow dot that can hold in it for me such a concentrated pinpoint of pain. We cry grief from outside of us into the inside of us because we need it. Grief is transferable. We get Dr. Frankenstein and Frankenstein's monster so confused because the difference between them is just a question of in which body the grief gets housed. I write these poems to give birth, to kill, to give birth to the one thing I promise will kill me.

INVISIBLE AND NOT INVISIBLE

A woman gives birth to identical twins. One is named Invisible and the other is named Not Invisible. One you can *not* see and the other you *can* see. The one you can *not* see is named Invisible. The one you *can* see is named Not Invisible. She raises both of them in a house. Though they are both always at her side and always at each other's side, she grieves for the one you can not see, Invisible. *O Invisible, O Invisible* she cries while looking at Not Invisible. After a while, it becomes difficult to tell them apart.

THE BLACK HOLE

When I show someone the black hole it is difficult for me not to push them into it. I'm not sure what that means but it frightens me. Sometimes when I go to the black hole by myself, I'm afraid I might jump into it despite my own resistance. I'm afraid of myself. It's as if I've been given someone else's heart and someone else has mine, as if our hearts had been switched while we slept. One day, when all the continents have been buried in ocean, we'll slowly float past each other in our little boats, hearing our own hearts in each other's chest, and watch each other like stars we don't know are dead.

DEATH LETTER

I get a letter in the morning that said the woman I love is dead, that she has been trampled by elephants. I haven't seen her in years, but I think about her every time I make the bed, every time I set the table. I think about how perfect we would have been together. When I arrive at her house with flowers to pay my respects, I see her in the window, dusting the sill. She isn't dead at all. She shows no signs of being trampled, even her clothes are starched and pressed. I knock on the door and she opens it. *You're not dead* I say. *Who are you?* she says. *What do you mean?* I say. *It's me.* But her eyes just squint at me as if I were microscopic. *Weren't you trampled by elephants?* I say. *No* she says. *There aren't even any elephants around here.* When I walk away, flowers in my fist, I think about all the different kinds of death. I wish she would have been dead just like the letter said. There is more truth in that kind of death, and I felt so much closer to her then.

SOMEONE FALLS IN LOVE WITH SOMEONE

Someone falls in love with someone but that person falls in love with someone else, and that person falls in love with a different person, and that person falls in love with someone else too. I am the third person and you are the fourth person. I am an ambulance driver and you are an ambulance driver. I am resuscitating someone in a basement and you are resuscitating someone else in the same basement. *Are you falling in love with someone else?* I ask from across the basement but you can't hear me. I am being strangled by the asphyxiated person who I am resuscitating and you are being strangled by the asphyxiated person who you are resuscitating. I hope this is it. I hope we all die just like this, in someone else's arms, young and beautiful and true.

THE PERSON WHO WAS EXPECTED

A man is sitting at a table. A woman says *can I sit with you?* The man says *sorry, but I am expecting someone.* The woman sits down anyway and says *I am your wife. No, no, you're not my wife, but you do look familiar* says the man. *I think I am your father.* The woman says *oh no, you're not my father, you're my son. Where have you been?* They stare at one another until the person who was expected shows up and hands the man a magic baby. It grows in his hands. Its hair spreads across the floor. This makes sense. The four of them live in the future where everything makes perfect sense under a blue crying beam of bird-light.

BRANDON SHIMODA

While visiting shrines in Japan—July-August 2011—I noticed hanging at the head of each inner altar a circular mirror. How bewildering, I thought, to have come all this way to see hanging before me a small reflection of the way I have come. But then instantly, No: the circle shone more of an eye than a mirror: beautiful, specific, but ultimately unfathomable. It was more perceptive of me than I of it, wherefore what was more truly hanging was *outside* the mirror. I tried to position my head in the circle, but only clouded colors and shadows availed. It wasn't until visiting a shrine in which hung a mirror that had been worn completely to stone that I felt a relation to where I was standing. *Figuratively we may say that every mind is a world of ghosts—incomparably more numerous than the acknowledged millions.* My first poems—also my last (or most recent)—were written at night, before sleep. On my stomach, glasses off, avoiding eye contact with the paper, I recall the day: words, images, old women, half-faces. Sometimes, as my body grows heavy and my consciousness with it, two voices arise, and begin speaking to each other. No again: they do not begin; they have always been, the volume gone down on the world. My task becomes to transcribe, without judgment. Inevitably, the pen falls from my hand, bleeds through the sheets. The moment is prohibitively brief. I equate the living of each day with what I am permitted of that moment, the evening oracle. *The books that I'm writing are houses that I build for myself.* I used to imagine writing to be the equivalent of entering a body of water—not diving or drowning, but *being lowered*—further from light to where all that had been lost or forgotten—especially occluded and erased—gathered: the pantheon. And yet, the dead do not belong to me; I belong to the dead. *Whosoever understands what human goodness is, and the terrible cost of making it, can find in the commonest phases of the humblest lives that beauty which is divine, and can feel that in one sense our dead are truly gods.* There are two graves: the ritual and the burial. The ritual is where the living commune with the dead, while the burial is where the body, or the body's relics, can be found, or lost forever. The two graves are often one, though more often the distance is wide. Which one is the book? Which one the poem? Both are reconstitutions—part act of will, part monumental error. And from a shadow the sound of deep laughter.

from LAKE M & EVENING ORACLE

A body of wood
bows forever away
past the darkened half

of the canyon
               coming
Arc and open

onto bodies'
        dissolving
Petals   I don't see

The wing of a small pond
In a daughter's hand
Days are meant to unfold

Or fold
Or fly or
Drowning, die

You see, there is something
Rare in the air or
Open, fits

One life
To it and that
Is yours, and you know it

And still
Don't care, the fight is
Over, that

Has been made clear, though
Not without
Enough. You went off

Your maiden, a billow
along the canvas wall, quietly

Worded against moments of shadow
          violently burned

     across   Your barracks

Have never been so
immaculate, yet

You've been scripted
to fold
and re-fold

Every detail
into every other, from dawn
until pre-dawn

How much of her is condensation on
your lens   The wish to wring
a pale, white neck

Etsuko paints faces on rocks
She finds
A simpler credulity

One rock wears a hat
With a pink stripe and a yellow stripe
Etsuko encountered in a major mountain system

One rock is a man, as such
Has a baby. It is the baby knows all
The world before him

One rock resembles a pig
A pig, Etsuko says, with a coquettish face
And peasant's bonnet

A sensitive and triangular face
In the mirror, a person deserving attention
A crystal used in magic

One rock resembles a warrior
Walking through a field toward the sea, blazed
By prior warriors

The sea is inhuman, how about you
Let me paint eyes on your nipple …
How many live there? How many used to?

Etsuko has rocks woven into her walls
Heavy, her house carries
Away

A face
Upon a rock, a gourd
A large fruit, prison clouds

Night fires, stars
The back of a neck
Painted with a free hand

Etsuko's rocks look good when catching
Rain, and when the rain
Pulls off

Fog encircling a mountain
Every eye small, but what is seen
For real? The song played at one's funeral?
A lovelorn feeling? No, the fog
Adult and expanding

One joins a cult
And loses touch
With those who disapprove
But they are lively, or so is said
They barely move

Masako runs the public bath
Sees everyone without clothes
Takes them all to bed, impressions made of
Loneliness and night, she hands out soap, razors, the paper
White towels, small things to bite down on

I gave Masako a copy of *O Bon*, the book I wrote
While dreaming of her, or the version of her
I was dreaming of
That brought me out of the dream
She touched it, said, Has *O Bon* thrown pain?
Has *O Bon* tricked anyone into thinking
Pain is not that, but that pain over there
While here I can suddenly move?
The fog has lifted—I can love and be loved?

I sit in the mint. My heart has a bubble
An old man tells me not to go in
Above my heart, I have gone in above my heart
I am white, the fog is judicious, the mountain
A splendor, but who will remember
What I looked like?
The old man
Cocks his head to stare into mine
I stare at his recumbent testicle

At night, you craft your figurine
    from stone

Gathering your maiden
into a porcelain gown
beneath a penetrant lamp

Her feet pristine, sharply white
arched to quiet in the hall

Fingers softly on your arm

A bridge of birds constrains her hair
bowed above her faceless head
each finery crest displaying

Lean in to carve her mouth
    a tiny craze across her cheek
Widening   *take me*

Before I am taken by the light

I climb on the nightstand, singing

A woman is planting spinach
In the ruins of her house
Washed away white
Circles each spinach

Each circle is heat
The woman's knees touch
Her house in the form fit to give, reappearing in
The waves—there are none; it is fall

People admire the woman
Planting spinach
Where her house once stood, her age is
Mistakable

The spinach is her destiny
She does not claim its admiration
She can be the substantiation of the devil
If she wants to

The spinach will grow
Will be picked and eaten
The spinach will keep growing, keep being
Picked and eaten, in each instance

The message is:
I was living
I will live
I live

The woman crouches
Without accent, an intestine among the waves
Packed with spinach, only
Partially digested

Destiny is nourished
Not the word, *destiny*, but *destiny*
Is embarrassed. It too is hungry, feeds on what is
Forthcoming, human hair and mildew

Whatever fits into the hand
Is what is encouraged to be taken
So take it—that is what the foreigners do
They live here too, they've lived here always

           I

  cut

your flesh

           I

        am

    the fence

The above are from three related series: *Lake M, O Bon*, and *Evening Oracle*. *Lake M* along the (contour) lines of my grandfather's imprisonment, and the internment of Japanese Americans, during the Second World War; *O Bon* within and for the mind and memory of my ancestors; and *Evening Oracle* over a period of two months in Japan (2011-2012), at night, in the beds of friends and strangers. The italicized lines in my statement are from Lafcadio Hearn and Etel Adnan.

Can't just sound good, has to be good (Johnny), got to be real, to be or (not) 2B—what is the question? Ask it, (a tisket a) task it, mask it (grins and lies); tell the truth slanted (not crooked), circuitous (not duplicitous). Do-it-to-it-us: we be black, Jes B. Semple, jes grew, simply, simile, smile!

I sing myself, and I quote myself: "In an era when young poets are routinely told that there is nothing outside the scope of poetry—nothing too mundane, nothing too unconventional—I would like to think that race is not an excluded or suspect subject. I would like to think that one's poetry—whether a single poem, a book, or an oeuvre—cannot be 'too black.'" I sing the body electric-chaired, charred, pepper-sprayed, bruise-hued, blackened. A seasoned American in an American season (fall, falling, fallen).

To be is not taboo: let it be salty, let it be bloody, let it be body, let it be risky, let it be alone (but don't let it be lonely). Study long (history), study wrong (injustice), study song (culture). *Sing a song of sixpence, a pocketful of rye, four-and-twenty lions and tigers and bears—oh, my!* When the needle skips a groove, it's still groovy. Grave-y. Trane.

My favorite things: when the line breaks, when the rhyme schemes, when the meta pours out of the images and gets the white space dirty. I take up form without fear or loathing—as Sonia Says: *the form will not deform me.* Or I embrace the prose and cons (fool me twice…). Or I make a shape that shapes the meaning.

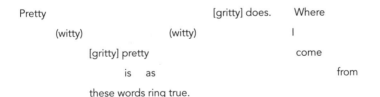

Walk into the smallest rooms of writing, the tiniest cells of language, and start pushing on the walls. Kick and twist until something slouches, marches, or itches to be born. Scratches. Hatches. Water that furious flower and watch it explode. The explosion is poetry. The fragments that remain are poetry. The (un-new) thing made (anew) from those scattered, jagged fragments is poetry.

A DARK SCRAWL

war can't amass a brass tack. war's
all bad acts and lack, scandal

>   and graft. watch flags clash and tanks

attack camps. arms crack—rat-a-
tat-tat!—and ban calm. cabals

>   plan vast land grabs and trash far-

away clans' shacks, pads, plants, halls,
and farms. war's fans track maps that

>   warp and adapt as rash hands

grasp at lands that attract. rag-
clad lads and gals gnaw small snacks,

>   catch-as-catch-can. war's gray days

last and last and, as man slays
man and clans fall apart, can

>   wax halfway banal. ask: what

attar can mask war's stank past?
what fragrant balm allay all

>   qualms and angst war spawns? alas,

sad mamas bawl, what wan dawn
shall mark war's last gasp? what art,

pray, shall patch tracts war ransacks,

mass and spark lads' and gals' war-
raw shards, and call glad days back?

LEGIT-I-MATE

legal measures gave us the rule of thumb.

antebellum legislation made a clean sweep

of lawful unions in certain quarters. some men

accumulate wives religiously, a practice which

frequently goes unstated. government outlawed

loving in virginia. a president once proclaimed,

ask not what your relationship can do for your country—

there's no telling. the marriages with the most

sanctity immigrate to the homeland with the most

security. *dear john, your proposition ate my california*

marriage license, so my honest woman can't make

an honest woman of me. fair trade act: the government

stays out of our bedrooms, and in exchange

our bedrooms stay out of the tax code.

there's been a separation of church and state,

but perhaps it's time for a formal divorce.

'THE PEOPLE WANT THE REGIME TO FALL'

      march, too, this year was nervy, making all
it could of winter's costume, flaunting snow
and sleet, slapping our stiffening cheeks cold
      and red, wearing white well past when it's called
      for, leaving the tree limbs smooth, the buds stalled
deep in their dreams, a too-static tableau,
everything with liquid in its veins so
      damn-near frozen, spring slowed down to a crawl.

      still, hope springs, we drink in every season,
and people take root, sprout, and blossom in
the capitol greens and the public squares
      in cities near and far. call it treason,
      if you will. i call it nature, human,
to forge an april from the heat of our desires.

STUDIES IN ANTEBELLUM LITERATURE, CH. 5
(OR, TOPSY-TURVY)

19th-century novels paint
quite the chromatic picture

of america—take the white
whale, say, or the scarlet

letter—but they aren't
all tarred with the same

brush. for comic contrast
some give us black humor:

national relief projected
onto one dark little head,

in turn projecting, in all
directions, a local choler.

     #   #   #

antebellum lit still tinges
tongues with shady tints.

our language is loaded,
packing heat, a weapon

concealed, it seems, only
from the blissful. who'd

say *x used to be a small*
college town, but then ten

years ago it just grew like
topsy? i'd say it grew like

kudzu, maybe. or like
wildfire. not like topsy.*

       * things that just grew
       like topsy: the middle

       passage death toll.
       the black prison

       population. the crop
       of negro spirituals. like

       crazy. like a weed. like
       a motherless child.

WEATHER OR NOT

time was on its side, its upside down. it was a new error. generation why-not had voted its con-science and a climate of indifference was generating maelstromy weather. we acted as if the planet was a stone-cold player, but turns out the earth had a heart and it was melting, pacific islanders first into the hotter water. just a coincidence—the polar bears are white and their real estate was being liquidated too. meanwhile, in the temper-temper zone, the birds were back and i hadn't slept—had it been a night or a season? the birdsong sounded cheap, my thoughts cheaper, penny, inky, dark. language struck me as wooden, battered. the words became weeds, meaning i couldn't see any use for them. i had signed my name repeatedly without any sign of change. i was still bleeding from yesterday's sound bites, and the coming elections were breeding candid hates by the hand-over-fistful. there'd been an arab spring, but it was winter all summer in america.

Poetry can sometimes be a hard thing to wear well. I find that I feel somewhat secretive about my practice. It's a bit like telling someone you are religious; you never know what they are thinking in that moment. The difference between a person that writes poetry on occasion and the born poet is the need to return to the poem, being mesmerized by a stain trapped in its wiring. The actual composing feels like a block of time I have paid for in advance, being warmly received and led to a clean room to have my way. No one else is watching but they can hear you, not through an overtly performative reading style per se. It's the crosscurrent rhythm of language, its ever-changing grip and daring release. An open valve of oil, blood flowers and jewels in retreat. A cage fight that envelops chance and no germ can survive in this light. It is dependent on an early fearlessness within forms, espionage and its attendant soundtrack. How to suffuse a few lines with more atmosphere than even a hall of mirrors could manage. So many natural gaps occur in my thinking in the heat of composition, sometimes the fact that a work is lyrical is totally lost on me. I'm listening to how the words exist as sounds next to one another before I latch onto their meanings. Charles Olson's line, "I have had to learn the simplest things last" has always been a comfort to me, as has Eileen Myles's more recent statement, "I'm not *not* a language poet."

DREAM

A curtain dragging gold rises on The Big Heat
Two words are fused to a blood-letting chain
How beautifully the brakemen allow the blood through
I rest on the slip of the black coral sea
Steel quilted in lines wider than the streets
Pinned as a wing or thin cord, that he summons
In order to drive us away, that glamour is an investment
Involving desire and unreality. The poems are perfect
Laid back time-machines, ground-blooming flowers
Their endless pastel grime in streaks
A blocking of my own in-expertise, a tunnel
Blown down past the marble to brass
And first to charge the shore, waving our shields
A castle left cooling to ruin
And the islands will flower in and out

ODE

Master collagist lover householder editor surrealist confidant, making magic pointed underpinnings on paper pulled through a typewriter, personal priest, follower, holed up in Cairo, stuffy small room you never want to leave, ballad airs, the only young woman I would love to be forced to make love to, BFF tennis stars together, he would bury his paintings, I think that had to be it, he was a better queer than most live ones too, lonesome traveller who would try everything and get mixed up after. He made private music, I spent more time with him than anyone,

a psychic who saw words or heard them or found small filthy objects on the street that came back as words, he loved poems more than graphite he used to make his works. A father and furious maker of a million books, poetry books made for birthdays, one copy, reading to his countess daughter. Hot punk ass, huge cock and personality, big mouth performance, amazing. The writer everyone co-opted sooner or later, it's the new pillow book, don't miss it, tree trimmer, painter of small square pastels, a Marlborough man, canadian coveralls, short short fiction,

printer of Expensive Magic and The Poems from The New Winter Palace, String Of Small Machines, shy guy, editor, spawn of dyke and fag, a real bully in Colorado Springs, father of one, I think people thought we were together at least once. Sad poems tracing the beautiful decline of Santa Cruz or any chinatown (seriously) he found love and stopped publishing so much, the best accidental poet and beauty consultant and dealer. Believer. Pissed off muslim-or that was the rumor. I would just drop in on him, he turned me onto Fielding Dawson, John Altoon and Charles Olson all over again.

Phoenicians. Long talks on there very possible establishments here to for unrealized. Cock-tease, very able writer and critic, portrait of Dorian Gray Steez. Impeccable evening, Hermes, answering the desk phone every five seconds, very generous, he gave me 20 dollars when I swept into town as a fake hustler (a thousand years) genius prose. In several bands and none to match his genius, he is not playing dumb, he's quiet, pimp of the year and maybe my favorite. Could you play me my last rights?

Torn paper film of a wolf mans romance and in the end he rises from the grave... or does his maiden? Joke Night. Opera plaza taking tickets. You're so good to me. You printed my secret ceremony next to a poem by the one I love. You bring half drunk bottles to parties, believer, curator. He said he was going to paint a house. He left me in bed where I watched LOADS, I think that he was hustling, thats what she said, his shows were tight and massive. He could appreciate a turn of phrase or lyric, threading the needle. I don't want to live without your love.

PARIS

I can disappear before your eyes killing you
I slay you with my eyes you disappear
That's how I would remember that line and How To Write
Actually, certainly, stupidly, only the ladies strumming language
They are not women, they are nights
Wrestling these lines off the back of a knife
They have a second life spent in stone and so attended
Bomb the bridge to heat my hands
Work their handlers in order
Go to the movies all day, only to collapse and focus
To finally hand off my faded flower
Caring and pointed, she brought me up and loosened my mind
Toward the checks and imbalances
And cameos in lucifers grotto.
I remember a full on scottish plaid suit
The gravitron, SEXODROME growing out of apollinaires grave
Empty balcony seats, operatic little fills
The poems of a Multi-billionaire, a vow of silence
Fine and Mellow, all the things you are

SIMPLE GIFT
on a painting by Bob Thompson

The mouth of the cavern
Is cut along the top like snowy peaks
In cartoons—it zigzags. I sweat onto
My violet shirt in the shape
Of a heart, lock that away
Behind varnish, a hidden floor
Between stalactites
      (long trick knives)
          A lady of Falconbridge & lady
Of Dorset
     Torn back
through. the center & made quiet
A paper cut black branch set
On a red field. A horse
Draws the carriage past a lake
Of blue & all the kinds
      Are laid down
In the forest to live
         Tilt their heads back
         Don't think of stopping
Your shooting, more drinking!
These are to be
        Among the permanent
     (wrong) colors
Ice rats in stairwells, above us
Centaurs (twins) smack their heads
Into light bulbs. They get excited
    Over massacre
    Who were once
  The innocents who never hoped
To live out unspoken prayer. A country

That laid dark so long
                    Pyramids send word
        To the painted mountains
                Don't try and lie down
            As it gets late. Stay on guard
Study your drums & then tighten, pound back
            A few shots more
                    Ash on the sea floors
Don't you scrape away too many organs
Or paint over.
                Do not temper the spirit.

i write, as the ancients would have it, like a bear. the saying goes like this: the mother licks the shapeless cub into something beary. ditto me as per the poem.

i want sound to be the grapple gear. the 777 living hands fanning forward in the nose of that thumbing mole.

i want the sound to lean, to touch, to spill. elbow of mercury.

see i wait for the sound to guide my body and for the little scenarios to open up. the slippy architecture of my in/process poem has all to do with bulge. i wait for the 'place' where sound bulges into the fevers of a scenario.

one climbs or descends the washy ladder until that longitude of the poem happens. once there i do what everyone does on 'level' ground. i rest a little. sound the rocks for snakes. guess at the laugh wrinkles on the stranger whose snack wrapper is buzzing in the overwintering berry area.

i used to make thin, ladderlike poems. some wider. often thin tho. these days they are widening.

maybe they're a little skeletal. the lie of the abandoned. after any one thing moves on then the next thing piles in. fieldmouse as the second 'heart' in the ribcage of the ditched 'deer.'

i have been told to use punctuation. to use uppercase lettering. in the schools of poetry one hears many things. that's fine. sometimes tweed creates some kinds of rashy telling.

for me, so far, poetry has maybe been about maybe making the same 'mistakes' again. maybe about learning to love the broken in my way of making things 'right.' i did not 'find my voice.' maybe i just kept on in my beautifully stupid jumpin' bean way. tho you'd have to be an idiot to orphan every semicolon on planet earth;;;;;;

see: the lie of the horizon. lo: the narrowing road is really truly wide as hell. call it learning to live with what my body makes. but not just learning to live. relishing. mustarding. in it. it. i am between the i and t with a beautiful bag of chips.

i used to say that i wrote poems so that i could perform them. but that's a lie. least a half moonspoon of ash in that fire. i write what i can how i can. from and through my body.

i have high blood pressure. my poems have high blood pressure. i squirm a bit in public. my poems squirm for always. my knees click like marbles on carpet foam. my poems click like marbles on...

and there's a country diction in there. a chatty urgency. these voicings mostly come from places. taylor and rusk county. that's northern wisconsin. they come of heading west on I-10 out of houston. come out of the powder coffee creamer smell of the slaughter yards in sealy texas in 1988, too.

i am young there. all yearn gear. kid flattening his cowlick with spit.

IN THE OLD DAYS REDWING BLACKBIRDS HEY HEY
PROPHESIED THE HEAVENLY GARDEN TOMATO

talkin fruit flight   talkin hearty sleeve

turned sod takes sun's lead
refuses sun's lead
what a lark a mouth
made of meat for meat
or the hairy ropes of cultured greens
or words or love ohh vague leases
on longitudinal certitudes

now turned sod so cold
now it's the dead not the ticking medium life trees
rattling the pennies around
in their skulls like wild birds in
snug houses about a month of
abandon away from drafty
and they die on the dusty floors
like crazy animal flowers grazing on
a crazy fleshy froth throb wind

now sun sot sod
so warm yes the dead write the hair
along the tender crisps
crests of your ears
far finger familiars are
lute goblins are aeolian laudanums
it's the bread of breath rising up
through the soils if you live then your breath
tunes your body to the temperature
of your breathing and the dead
cradle your breaths armfuls of loaves of nose and mouth

and no one yells loathsome remonstrations
when the beautiful youngen
drops five staffs in the common dusts
where men with sex sores have washed
their cast iron linen their mouths leather cups
their teeth luckless dice wham or the fat
bones of fat mice fumble
with the numbers inkwells in the corners
a deeper goldener cheese somehow
lifted from the tensed steeled snap function
can steal all that you can carry
when there's nobody at home in your bones
cept the one root cellar toad's one least pancakey sprung gong
and then someone beautiful in killingly beautiful massacred jeans
someone perfectly alive
because salted with a sugar impatience
spirits a saltshaker into the garden

and the two of you hand-dine on maters
after the apple fashion
pass the shaker back and some kind of thoughtful

an everyday salt exchanged
as tho the last few morsel bits
of meat on earth after everything burns
burns or drowns the two of you on
on or under a teetery plank
was once a vital keeper of the weather war off

to turn your wrist on
like this
frames the sweet
in saving's saline sands

argues against
whiskery deserts
little glistering seeds these
ride as like albino lice
mmm some juicy alibi
in a wet cheat dream

good-night your chin blinds is blinding
that's a little glass ghost spitting
something like window skid on your chin
yes future water mmm all over your chin

a body can't help it it takes us away across
the lawn back the ground gives under foot until it won't because it can't
and then the canting stairs
the seesaw heehaw speech-heel stairs
quoth weed phrase like

eff u chainsaw tongue and yr mechanical yodel rationing
raffling steel
eff u too to the bearded porkmouther's
soda pop teeth waggin like the balls of a buck
runnin for his life for to yell floor-to-ceilin tin pan brrrr

people wear the
invisible touches of others
all their lives
and that is such a beautiful thing

a forgotten shaker in a garden also so beautiful

sun on top slop buck missionary
metal hat space
chubby elbow eggs

fried eggs
rise up all
water muss and mess around

sun yes lakes
the smallest thing everything
it what it stretches
fish going ahh
at the fish dentist mm
mm long shine in

inn a way we live in a world where dryads
just after dark enough
drop from trees from the darkening trees
sage smudges or oat burn
blind spots in the birth race to the hospital

slate the salt for removal
happen sugar pillar by morning

can't quit frog love crying
that swamp patch spring fed
too well seconds thirds help me
ooh wheat walrus honey
when chairs went corn easy
was the beginning of the end of the world

depends on how the button eye
on how the thread twangs on deeper
back in there tell me sing it is that a rut
yr browning yr best britches in
or art thee the noodling champ of the world

mmm routine'll jazz a bean
ritual mama yeah has a nice ring
try oxbow beaver drover drooler roarer of
a tree ain't a tree til it stops the water
with its felled self naturally

all in i am for finding
that these these are our footprints
and broken branch bits and browned
to a sweetness the human mouth has
forgotten how to love
yes it looks like least an hour
beyond the language of the picnic
for 'our' apple 'core'

kick it
tern feather white it horsey nostril exhale
the transom and whorl of dust
no one ever has been lost has been on a road
you are wearing
in a skin cradle
behind your right ear
and riding there

ah easy as air without wind or oh
the fox's breath in the fox's dream
of the fire walker man-of-stoning it towards
his day job so much trip stiffness
until one warms into the working
and then it's like swimming
and then it's like milking
the eyes of the kinder dead
to repaint these rooms

CHRISTOPHER STACKHOUSE

There is something ghostly, disturbing, elegant, and stupid about any effort toward creativity. Things are born for variable and no particular reason, and here we sit watching a screen, alluding to some desire to connect, but having such lust, potential friendship, a drink shared and story swapped mediated by yet another effort to insert ourselves in the confusion of death, or less harshly said, the brevity of attenuated bloodlife, which we find in our speech, in our acts of love, in our minor, casual, discreet daring to be ourselves among so many other desperate selves: with that I have to ask, What is a poetics? What is philosophy if it is not being? How much spectating must we do before we find ourselves formed enough to stand confidently a part of, or be comfortable within, the one miracle we know well to be our conscious selves? I am still nevertheless interested in a good painting.

ANGEL SMOKE

angel smoke reduced to mirage on the glass,
each convex reflection, separately throws corpulent light,
the moment thin as parchment, sparing the goat—
scholars orient beauty around a specific symmetry,
difference apparent between being shown, being seen—
a red deficit: "The skin of the scrotum looks like
the skin of a prehistoric animal," she says, takes a drag—
two stones in the shreds making headway, change in the mouth

THE ARTISTS, THEY WANT TO SIT IN A ROOM TOGETHER

The artists want to sit in a room together,
talk and not talk, about the wars around them.

In the fashion of artists, they sip, nibble, pine
for arguments sake, the variations of yellow.

Today, a bourgeois moment each protean conn-
oisseur howls a coloratura, promising not to
forget photos of the amputee, an erotic thong.

Their bricolage forged, available in unlimited editions.

2:49 PM

Poetic communion, something like that, while everyone else is taking care of business, at 2:49 pm my day has already been longer than most people have been alive. Whatever we're trading would be fine enough if I could just stop crying long enough to say I've had enough of this constant leaving. It is not like I haven't proven I am chronically alone. There's nothing particularly special about that. All these adjectives you keep telling me I use too often, as if I didn't already understand how clearly my vocabulary is so impoverished. You're smarter than me I suppose. We are not the science of money, architecture of an emotional life, or balance of sensibilities. We are something simpler. At least that's what I've been told. For more accuracy I look at my daughter's drawing on the desk, which she has titled "A butterfly in 100 blades of grass." That's action on the calendar. A glass of milk. A sedative. Even she knows well the productive use of longing.

THOUGHT AS TUNING FORK

Turn about candy wrapper tumbling peach colored in the air…

Careen toward, passing numbers, one, a vellum spread to few…

Roofing darkness is faint noiselessness; housed there is unnamed hue…

What hurts more than desire is more… Just ask Cynthia…

Wearing less than silver rain, silent aggregate, peels an empty lane…

Thrust to wit, bargaining her patent launches coil deep inside the cortex resides…

Equivalent, green hair heaving in our skins grows erect, hanging wet…

Up to the moment parting trees, dashing child, with arabesques, moving in…

Marble thought if that means anything, swirl. Place a blue tab on the page…

Shelter is brown. Just think about it. Cage as grail. Thought as tuning fork…

ON THE PRECIPICE OF WATER

A flower petal on the rear top of the toilet seat
testing the brink, cream and violet, clearly
a petal casting a shadow on the water. Just before
the white Bordeaux on the kitchen table,
gold liquid in a bottle. The dog moves
in the living room chewing a bone.
I can hear it tapping the floor.
Surely, the neighbors below can hear it tapping the floor.
The dog, chewing the bone. Pacing toward her
past my girlfriend's cello, just before
intruding on the soft appendage contemplating
a fall from the shaded precipice in to the water.

MATHIAS SVALINA

0. Crazy Spirit's Train

1. The Pharcyde's Runnin'

2. Sissy Nobby's Nothing On You

3. Ozzie Smith

4. Carole King's Way Over Yonder

5. A Silver Mt. Zion's There Is a Light

6. Pallbearer's Foreigner

7. Emperor's I Am the Black Wizards

8. Boards bent beneath books

9. Matana Roberts's Pov Piti

10. That photoshop of Lil Wayne chillaxing with Garfield

11. Julie Mehretu's drawings

12. Remedios Varo's Creation of the Birds

13: Agalloch's Black Lake Nidstång

14: A black seed (from an apple?)

15. Cumin on the palm & Paul Westerberg's Meet Me Down the Alley

16. The dust one must brush off cardboard boxes

17: Two teeth broken off so far

18: Foreigner's Juke Box Hero

19: The Body's A Body

20. Skip James's Special Rider Blues

21. That totally jacked ermine in Da Vinci's Lady with Ermine

22. He-Man

23. John Coltrane's *Ascension*

THE WINE-DARK SEA

I reach for the kerosene of stars.
For a fragile dictionary.

Anything: umber, sickness,
self or harm.

This is a geyser religion.
I'm just the bagman.

THE WINE-DARK SEA

I want to answer questions,
what the date wants
from its box,
printed in
lip.

The concerto
cast a morning
on me beneath
all the bridges
where all the ropes dangle.

I cannot stand
inside myself.

What emerged
when I opened my mouth
was a thanking tomb.

So we tremble.
Do we tremble?

We tremble.

THE WINE-DARK SEA

I am trying
to be simple as ink.

I talk to you
sometimes
in the daylight.

At night
I try not to
suspend.

I hope it does not
distract you.

There is so much
I can't form
that is true.

Celan said this
to Liana Shmueli:

Through you I translate you over to me.

THE WINE-DARK SEA

In these holy days
of ditch & feast,

of the festival
of spines,

I bless
the festival.

THE WINE-DARK SEA

Two doors stand open
piles of crumbs
before each.

I knew you
in the days of sky.

A no-name hour.
A no-name sky.

The sea, wakeless, rises
daily from the dead

in the trembling
of the dumbstruck again-today.

My work shapes a desire to broaden the potential readerships with which contemporary writing can interact, insofar as I see poetry as the primary location for engaging predicaments of global citizenship, transnational relations, namely those of Latin America and the United States, the political emotions of sexual difference, and Latino-a identity. In that process, I take cover only as I am seen hiding in the figure-field relationship. I want two sets of things: those pertaining to an alleged home and those evicted from it; avant-garde truth only as it is found in its distortions, and as a proxy for other enjoyments. In works that address material culture, the object of art, and the dreamtime of the seeable, I submit tactics and metaphors, stratagems and voices structured into displays that overturn the pyramids of high and low. In idioms at once popular, elite, disciplinary, and insubordinate, my desire is attuned to how habits and language can galvanize individuals into cultural actors. Along the way, poetic space doubles for a self in the talking cure; and junk economies of sensorial overload foreshadow globalized duress. The settings travel over time and geography: a lens that telescopes from the transatlantic colonial project into the perspective of contemporary art. Visually, with an object-based idiom that gleans only transitory insight, I seek poetry restless in its relation to the culture concept, and the image environment's relation to the letter—verbal performances that are paramount for surviving the onrush of historical change.

FREEWAY 1

As much velocity as there are seasons of reward and goodwill, as little comfort
eligible when the contours elevate and cradle, as many loyalties

connect to the pivot and pulses or as little light on two nations meant
all times to be failing or as yet to succeed   practical joke played as early

as the epigrams and flags for the priorities of leaving hoisted as late as
the death of a mood no one can really tolerate the pillar for posting

the crocodiles each cycle to cycle in drift and drag for historic view
claiming part and parcel at large in unflinching sweep the dinosaurs

and cosmonauts the glass refracted flash of exception chalk insoluble flex
or fidget the plan anathema   pliant volume   upended enclave of obtuse

enumeration or probable dissolve of the noblesse oblige complicit in
recline and ashes dormant   combustible unknown to certify provision

ah my refundable appeal to policy on the grounds set forth administrations
consistent with the standards, constituent of all these immunities

but evocative of language that, having so made a pact with the night examples
as to indwell its daylight haunting, emerges in accounts undaunted

lines venturing to outdistance description if they are to comprise what they
evidence. It's no endeavor confirming the laws of physics—merged lanes

that double for hunger and time: memorial to deter the varieties abridged

OR WHY THE ASSEMBLY DISBANDED AS BEFORE

Hosanna in the borderline cinderblock warehouse, as much applause
as possible to collapse inside an ambulance now that conveys

The intravenous bags and bottle holder, twenty-seven stones
from here to the Idyllwild   to the gun fields

It's a place you find automaton nurses who labor
in green-grey subterfuge, in all-over stripes

A round of punches to the lower jaw for my part in the main
so I get it now I'm the chosen one for reassignment

Face so altered as to beguile. This is enemy-convenient
a purview suitable to very new cosmetic methods.

Question is the admin diazepam and other hypodermics
were they counteractive or now consistent

With enough cases as to compel canvassers to anticipate
first signs of panic, sleepwalker antecedents

Tray tables in upright position, crushed ice out of open
mouth, air-conditioned ward redolent of superstores

And tattoo shops, or was it morphine sulfate in protocols
applied to disable the congenital twins?

Here's the world news: to junk-science prizes wax-candy
lips intone a flawless if always accented sentence

The kind of talking from another world where my mother
was Marlo Thomas and there were rival techniques

Contributed to the celebrity of my seven-sided disappearance
or was that all my enuresis when I doubled in size

As from her pocketbook, adorable but already diminishing?

VANISHING

Amulets that share a kinship in the histories of light and language when I unite the number 9 to 27, the word *tangerine* to *lemongrass, meadow spur* to *thistle, glimmer* to *destello*; drive that fades, splinter of duration evanescing; double life conjured by vocables from a zone of repetition—[mm]—its glow at the origin, vision contingent at the level of the letter—[ll]—all things abrupt now intermittent. Claims singular never less than overstatement, when I slip into view out of

joint with experience, when attributes of bliss and cataclysm reside not in portentous totality, but in the ordinary detail, attention requisite for me to tell the narratives of sight and sound in transformation. Discrete words a partial view, but even as I surface— subject to predicate, at best a proposition, belated reason "I" am the cause of my thoughts—why, in the domains of the ether, in the pharmacology of everyday matter, in the flattened contours, my singular life a social

statistic—is the charm not of narrative consequence, bestowed on me a script of action as to navigate the intangible space of so much undigested information? Rip in the web of meaning when I cast and draw, but owing to that gash where to see is to know, am I careful in my unwanted thought, in desires for such a gesture as to embolden, persuade? Limberness, untangle the strict partitions without hazard to the shell protective of

all persons provisional in settings that reflect, I cover a ground, I quicken, I substitute the vanishing with constituent parts, regenerate, deprived of a halo, released from this fixity, am I not without radiance of my convenient forgetting and, everyday—because it so beckons—in the recurring custody of a world, around whose mindfulness we congregate, and over which we are inclined to argue?

I have a master's degree and I finally have health care. I consistently pass as a man and I am the safest I've ever been in my life. I started a project called *Made for Flight* and for that, I visit schools, youth groups, etc., and talk about trans identities, violence, how to be an ally. I am constantly saying these words: *A trans woman (usually a trans woman of color who is a sex worker) is murdered every other day worldwide.* Does saying this change anything? What does it mean to be complicit? When Janet Mock says, *Every time there's a trans woman of color in the media, she's getting killed. It wrecks our souls.* To whom or to what is she pointing? Can we separate self-hatred from the self? What does it mean, as a person who has already, in the minds of many, gone too far, to go too far? Where is excess and what does it clean? Do the dead women give a goddamn about all of those kites?

As a trans writer (and this is different, I think, than a writer who happens to be trans), I am particularly interested in form. Formally, *On the other side of the wall is a bench, after Basho*, is an experiment with passing and the act of confession. Now that I look like the guy who would tell those jokes, is he in me? Am I in him? Is this an act of violence? Who is the perpetrator? Who is safe? Who is seen? I expect folks to be uncomfortable with the work. I am uncomfortable with the work. It is, in a very visceral way, a grappling with implication, anger, blame, the line between shame (as Brene Brown defines it, "I am bad") and guilt ("I did something bad."). Something passes. And then, hopefully, something slips.

I think of the textual body as a gendered body. These massive prose blocks are a major shift for me and lately I've come to see them as mirroring my current gender expression in that they seem so coherent from a distance—using all of the devices of prose but then the text is unreliable; the veneer of coherence and safety completely gives way. The narrative is ruptured. How passing, for me, can be both a protection from violence and can perpetuate violence. A necessity and necessarily enigmatic. A practice of practicing. A reckoning with constraint, with ambivalence, and with form.

Also, I wonder: Is confession a form of intimacy? Is rejection? Is intimacy why violence exists?

ON THE OTHER SIDE OF THE WALL IS A BENCH
after Basho

I. the desert in june

the waffle house on the north side of the phoenix art museum has been converted into a thai restaurant and lisa and i are sitting across from one another in sticky red booths. we're looking through her new pocket pema when the thai iced coffee arrives. i don't need it and i feel kind of ashamed that i ordered it—the color of sand and seriously, ineffably sweet. my compression shirt, the new one, the one that tweaks my shoulder every time i take it off—it's sticking to me and i'm pretty sure i stink. my tits are on my nerves. my thighs keep touching each other. i wish i didn't hate everything about myself right now but i do, especially the way my belly pushes out when i breathe.

II. things that leave a clean feeling

the man who admits he fucks babies. the number of children born with syphilis in Baltimore, 1995-1996. fruit bats. a woman on the front porch eating breakfast. grass that can't get dry. an upside down mason jar on the shelf separated from its gold plated lid. a cow. a white cow. a white cow and the human hand above it. a white cow and the human hand above it held on film. names. nails left in the wall by the old tenants. the way a face looks when it is finally forgotten. a tooth in the dirt. a belt. a paddle. the window one closes too carefully. the window one can't wipe clean.

III. After driving 3,595 miles, my windshield wipers, it is determined, are utter shit.

My sister gets married. A drunk guy at a hotel asks me if I'm an artist and then wants me to decorate his car. Corn is everywhere. I hide out and I masturbate in my room. Facebook makes me feel bad about myself and so does Grindr. I delete each from my phone and then add them back on 17 different occasions. I go to two different big box stores in Minneapolis to buy a book called *The Gifts of Imperfection* by "researcher/storyteller" Brene Brown. I sleep in a tent. Nervously. A friend's partner is pregnant but she thinks she is miscarrying when I visit. There is blood and we don't use the word baby, or rather, we feel weird about using the word baby when what we mean is fetus because we've always been staunchly pro-choice. My back hurts. The TV is on. We are happy when the baby is ok. I ride in the back of a truck every opportunity I get. I read *Babyfucker, 100 Notes on Violence*, and *Bad Bad*. I hike with Cara Benson and she tells me she's writing a book called *Cara Benson*. Bed bugs happen. Again. I spend a lot of time looking at lists of dead people. I don't miss anyone. Things change and I decide not to leave the people I love. Renay says, *everything should be epic*. I plagiarize parts of *The Power of Habit, Artificial Love*, and *The Compass of Pleasure* in every conversation for weeks.

IV. Melissa Dawn Tolbert

It always begins this way. To try to solidify one thing by wandering around in a field. To gather sticks. Trees are necessary. The field would be more accurately called a yard but yard implies boundaries, a fence. To place the sticks in any sort of geometrical configuration, to determine proximity simply by defining place, one need not have an understanding of physics, architecture, or strength. One can simply pile the sticks. It would be ideal for them to be about the same length. As is often the case, girth is relevant really only in relation to length. One could always break the sticks. There is nothing that says one has to use the sticks exactly as they are found. One could be methodical or not, careful or less so, it doesn't matter really. The field is ubiquitous. It's closer than one might think.

Have you ever taken a bundle of dry spaghetti and held it over a pot of boiling water with both hands? There is a certain satisfaction there. To break a singular thing that is also plural. To think one knows, but not really, what will happen next. Inevitably, a little mess is made. Individual pieces slip through, break unevenly, stab the wrist. One cannot help but imagine the pressure required, although vertically, to snap a human neck. Pressure is the wrong word. The word one wants is tension. A pulling force. A subtler mess. This is not the same as, say, dropping a glass jar, either intentionally or otherwise, from counter height, say 3-4 feet (no more than 48 inches) onto a Saltillo tile floor. All that sauce everywhere. The dog must be called. She's deaf but call her anyway. Here, dog. Look what we gave you on the floor.

When the dog was found she was pregnant. No one could tell really. She was young. Self-sufficient. She wasn't what one would call motherly. One could see how she would fight getting fucked by that one dog or any of the others, even if she was in heat. No one ever says this about pregnancy but gestation becomes aggression from the inside. That little thing would absolutely kill her if it could. And then it's over. It's almost like watching a woman take a shit. Humans are only one of three species who fuck outside of the ovulation cycle. Who engage in foreplay. Who, it could be argued, actually ask to get raped. Humans are also only one of four species who engage in monogamy or serial monogamy. Apparently this developed because the human brain, at full maturation, is around 1200 cubic centimeters whereas a woman's cunt, even on a good day, can only stretch to something like 400 cc. Something had to give either way. So, baby humans are born with severely underdeveloped brains covered by 44 separate bony elements. Crushing a skull would take considerably more pressure than snapping a bundle of dry spaghetti, although crushing a child's skull must be somewhere in the middle range. Still. That must be something one could accomplish on one's own. Just one person, just two hands.

One time, on a wilderness trip, a woman took a red apple, picked off the stem, and turned the apple upside down. She hooked her thumbs into the crevice that leads to or comes from, depending on how you think about it, the core. She was showing off, this woman, but people gathered, and she broke the apple clean in half that way. There was a guy who couldn't believe it (there's always that guy) and he took his own apple and basically squeezed the hell out of it. Pressure, not tension. He turned his apple into mush. The thing about a child's skull is the soft spot. It would make sense to hook one's thumbs there, to wrap the fingers around the jaw, to pull, to pull harder, to be impressed by the pulling, to not know how not to apply force.

Adult skulls are different.

In the field there is a freestanding wall. It's rectangular and one made of cinder blocks. From this distance the most arresting feature is the rusted open window. When a wall is decorative it is often made using a pattern called stretcher bond. Decorative walls cannot support any other walls and even the bench is a cosmetic bench. But how much weight could the open metal window hold? The wonderful part about hanging something is that gravity is what does all the work. If architecture is the belief that one is a different person depending on one's surroundings, one should consider more closely who one is over or under, one should experiment with force. Actually, there are two walls. There is no foundation for either of them. There is the wall you see and then there is also the wall that exists.

If there is only one story, it is inevitable that it will be repeated. One wakes up in a room and the fan is on. One touches one's body, comes to understand that one is not dead. Inferential logic is thought to begin in the dorsal root ganglia while habit loops are formed in the basal ganglia (a core structure shared across vertebrates). These loops are delicate. The car backs out of the driveway and pulls onto the interstate. It slows down next to a stranger. It signals for the next exit. To say that machines are animals is not at all to say that animals are really just machines. When David turned on a tank of nitrous and ran the tube into a mask he then pulled over his face, it was the machine that was the last one to hold him. Pleasure is a universal drive although the theory used to be that the body would do anything just to avoid pain. When the ventral tegmental area (VTA) is active it emits dopamine-releasing axons into the nucleus accumbens, amygdala, dorsal striatum, and prefrontal cortex. But it's the medial forebrain bundle, which is connected to the olfactory region, that sets off the VTA. Those who work in hospitals say they can smell death coming. Mallard ducks have a well-documented history of necrophilia, both heterosexual and homosexual. One researcher in the Netherlands witnessed the rape of a corpse that lasted an entire 75 minutes. It would be inaccurate to say one can become addicted to power or alcohol. Or even orgasm. The only drug the body recognizes is dopamine.

V. Sketches from Byrdcliffe

Why Apples Can Cause Riots: A Discussion of Linh Dinh's "Eating Fried Chicken."

Mad Cartographer: A Discussion of Jack Spicer's "Psychoanalysis: An Elegy."

Also, one bowl of Raisin Bran and four tablespoons of apple cider vinegar each day.

TC TOLBERT

VI. A record of poems I didn't write

I can't stop thinking about Pema Chodron. She said, "Everything that human beings feel, we feel. We can become extremely wise and sensitive to all of humanity and the whole universe simply by knowing ourselves, just as we are." I want this to be the one thing that someone else said that is true.

What's worse than having a husband with fashion sense? Knowing he looks better in your clothes than you. What's worse than picking up a hot blonde at the bar and having erection problems? When she doesn't. What's the best thing about fucking a transvestite? When you reach around, it feels like it's gone all the way through. What do 9 out of 10 people enjoy? Gang rape. What's the biggest crime committed by transvestites? Male fraud. What's the best part of punching a transvestite in the face? You get the pleasure of punching a woman but with none of the guilt. What do you call a tranny wrapped in aluminum foil? A TV dinner. How do you stop a tranny from choking? Take your dick out of its mouth. How do you make a dead tranny float? Take your foot off of its head. Why did the dead tranny cross the road? It was chained to a bumper. What bounces up and down at 100 mph? A tranny tied to the back of a truck. What's the difference between a dead tranny and a trampoline? When you jump on a trampoline, you take your boots off first. What's better than raping a dead tranny? Killing it first. What's worse than a having sex with a dead tranny? Having sex with a dead tranny filled with razor blades. What do you get when you dislocate a tranny's jaw? Deep throat. How do you make a tranny cry twice? Rub your bloody dick on its wig. What's the difference between a dead tranny and a Styrofoam cup? A dead tranny doesn't harm the atmosphere when you burn it. What do you call a dead tranny wrapped in a carpet? A fruit rollup. What do you get when you cut a tranny with a straight razor? An erection. What's the worst part about a gang rape? Waiting your turn.

VII.

things that pass

816 women who were not always women.

320

things that want to be quiet

from the time I was 6 months old until I was 3, my grandfather would pull his hardening dick out of his pants and rub it all over my mouth. John McPhee's critique of mimicry in urban America is really an assessment of landscape. universal design is misanthropic. even the best habits emerge without our permission. right now I'm in public and my nipples are hard. I want to rub them. I want to lift up my shirt and show you my incredible tits.

things that repeat

mirror neurons invite us to feel empathy for other human beings and often encourage us to smile when someone else is smiling. the idea is that this prevents us from hurting further those who have already been touched. ferdinand ambach visited new zealand from hungary. in december 2007, the 32 year old went to a bar and met 69 year old ronald james brown. we can never take it personally. none of it. I let a person strangle me once during sex not because I liked it, I don't, but because on the other side of the wall is a bench. some days, it's easy to feel decadent. on the way back to brown's apartment, brown confessed to playing the banjo. ambach, a diving instructor, understood the importance of breath. scientists used to believe it was the ability to use tools that separated us from other animals. now the difference is four-fold. surface tension allows objects heavier than water, such as spiders and paperclips, to distribute their weight and therefore feel supported by something they don't ever have to love. gay panic is a legal defense. ambach beat brown with a red instrument. in the average human body there are approximately 12 pounds of blood. the theory of "creative destruction" posits that even widespread societal gain always produces losses for some. when it was sufficiently broken, ambach shoved the neck of the banjo down the old man's throat. excess is a practical concern. oxygen is only one kind of touch.

IX. "Dick will make you slap somebody."

Of all of the things I am evangelical about.
I believe these things are probably true.

I am going to crib my poetics statement from Adra Raine, who wrote me a little while ago about a conversation the two of us had with Linda Russo on the way back from the Orono conference. Adra said: "You were speaking about 'not knowing what you are doing' when you are in the middle of a project, and that it isn't until later that you can look back and speak about it. And so I asked you why you trust the source, presumably 'in you,' that produces this mysterious thing. And... your response was to exclaim, 'I don't trust it! I don't trust it at all,' because you acknowledge that there are all kinds of cultural and social and political forces speaking through you, that ideology is impervious to one's wish/will to transcend it and speak from some 'other' center, and so your job is not to trust what you express but to make it visible/audible" in its untrustworthiness.

THIS IS A FUCKING POEM

don't expect too much.

Well I expect you to go into the
fucking human tunnel
I'm going.

pink grimy glossed
entabulature, welted
and tattooed. Enfolded in
ropy ceiling-hangings
but it isn't a room,

and bumblingly sliding
out, little legs of

a little girl, bum on the wall/opening

pink legs sticking out like a
hermit crab's, she's coming!

shudder out the little-girl
legs with a little
girl head mostly eyes, no ears,
bug brain, aimless

Send her to school

It's cold, and where should she
go, she will eat her
legs with her mandibles

her eyes will retract inside.

Stroke her riding hood
Settle down, little

nobody will hurtcha

by breaking off your little legs,
six little legs,
if you come.

RAIN COG

One who could not smell came up to the other's apartment (threw pebbles at the window) after the other had masturbated. The other not having washed her hands brought one a beer. One was intimate with the other's smell and wanted to be intimate with the other and was and did not know it. *That* old factory.

NOT DRUNCK AT ALL ANOTHER FUCKING LYRIC AMTRACK HUDSON–PENN

If you are in exactly
The same mood as me
When you get this
The poem is a fascist

Desire, ok
Because impossible like
Beating interiority out of exteriority
Which *would* clear a channel

It is the river I agree with snow
To reflect so
Much makes me opaque
In drydock give up sail

UNCLANG

I would like never to be obscure. I understand why I was: explaining
is a bore, and flattens lang, so, it takes experience to write a real poem
that is well-lit. Which is not the same as clear
drinking water from a jar, old
babydoll in bed. Broke and well-fed.

Lying here is great, I said,
you are not, nowhere, stay yup alnight.
You sunshine bleat.

I coulda moved to _____ moved to _____. My more glamorous avatar did, she willy
did, but when she was there, lookout, she looked in her pocketbook at the mirror
in the snapshut clamshell, the mirror was distwatted
curved along the shell wall. A weirdo pronunciation from New Ywok,
distwatted. That's just dis toy bin and it's more exciting than the fucking infernet.

Writing a poem is like reaching two prosthetic limbs out as far as you can on either side
to grab something in front of you. You can't grab it but maybe you'll take flight.

But I'm not trying to grab anything in front of me when I write a poem.
GET that kitty.

I'M TOTAL I'M ALL I'M ABSORBED IN THIS MEATCAKE

I gave you a sentence, can't back it with po-lice
Can't back it with any conviction at all

That frees me to say any lie I develop
That frees me of meaning and of consequence

I heard that prayer's efficacious on flowers
Long-distance or local, prayer helps make them grow

I submit that I had better mean what I'm saying
"I'm not the one saying it" "just writing it down"

Well who then is saying it. Trucks in the offing,
finch on the phonewire, movement of tree.

I'm not stupidly assailed by the moonlight
I'm an example, an experimental

Attempt to assess how a kid of my talents
Responds when she's given the life that I was

I'm the control and experiment bothly
you'll never get a result out of me

My guilt is omnipotence erupting backwards
heartbeat spans outward rebuffed at the skin

I'm total I'm all I'm absorbed in this meatcake
If I did all I could you'd shut up/be glad

Like fingers of a hand we all act as one
and aren't always needed, aren't needed as all

Ardent, hopefully astute, lover of the world's (so-called) sugar-junk & child of the long ago collapse of high & low, in poetry, I use my life's material as dream does though in this night it feeds music toward blundering points in the hard social mist where dear reveries are forced into a beauty sleep, & nightmares have insomnia which keep them up to labor (hunt & kill).

A Notley-an, member of the cult of John Wieners, as well as an apprentice to the unfinished opening New Narrative (Glück, Boone, Bellamy, Killian, Roy, et al) has pried & pries still, these keystones offer me not only models of potential but something inexhaustible the writing may converse with, dance to, flee or too closely inhabit for comfort, depending on the spell that has come over me that day, all of it charged most of all by the brilliant demands of work by peers & friends, as well as by other antecedents too numerous to list here though that vastness must be (gladly) marked.

Of equal importance is the work of pop composers & performers & producers. Again, there's an excess (the matter of poetry) of crushes & idols, but that varied/static form, of sweet nothings & unyielding contradictions, helps me touch & think & feel the world-system where my dream/writing life goes down, forged to so many degrees as I am by economy, yet not reporting everything of being to its score.

So one sings against & gets along & goes, perhaps with friends, arm & arm vexed by all the tears & deaths & births this teen Century, darkened by the power surge the gone one shot through fragile circuits, yields as a glimmering network of residual dominions & great liberation plots—public hyper privatized, asymetrically tyrannical, famed for brute force, glamorous, haunted by enchantment, made from poverties it is, in its adolescence, the young fact the old system grows old in, the dying patriarchal-money-race hate-time dominion-war form mistake it is such a joy to see staggering around on its last legs.

It hurts my ears to hear, how loudly, in "jubilant horror" (Ted Berrigan), the times call for poetry. How time's call is that & what we do. As such, my suspicion of received foreclosures substantiated variously by technocratic fallacies or the extrapolation of certain ontologies into walled-off ultimations gives my thought sites of fertile argument, creating enlivening frictions, beams of transport & intramural tensions which serve as leverage & keep the drink fresh.

Sometimes, one types up thought on all this stuff into a quantum window, & pressing send, makes the poem, feeling it so hard how dear a thing it is, that anyone would ever dream to listen to an other, where the miracle is, in the attempt to not cancel who one sings to. Thus to really really hear, & to be sung. We try & fail, & call as well that way the poem. Listening is writing. It hurts & caresses my ears. Can you imagine all the crazy abashed pleading emails with their valentines & cold agendas moving through the years, all the broken melded longing, the lost & found friends, voluminous piecemeal social epic better than the Moderns ever pictured it the way it makes me want to laugh & cry. The pop song's there, the poem. Just kids.

There's this clip of Duke Ellington, the interviewer asks him, "Where did you get all your ideas?" & he says, with warm but sure dismissal of the premise, "Ideas? Oh man. I got a million dreams. That's all I do is dream. All the time." Then the interview says, "I thought you played piano?" & Duke says, "This is not piano; this is dreaming." Then he plays a little bit, looking over at his band mates who dream back at him, joining in, making music with their instruments (material & limit which for me means body/death) exceeding & expressing what they bring from their existence to the wakening dream, achieved together & alone.

"That's dreaming," he says one more time, still playing as he says it, & then the thing fades out without them stopping.

from THE CRISIS OF INFINITE WORLDS

Krystle
Krystle Cole
you're all I thought about sometimes
I watched you while our daughter slept
your Sissy Spacek ways
your laconic demeanor in relaying
either ecstasy or trauma
& the un-embittered empathy your voice conveyed
on YouTube
which is our loving cup
the solution of butter
& DMT you took
anally that really made you
freak the fuck out
& your friends just stood there
watching you
as you hurtled alone through mirrored tunnels.
It's that frictionless feeling
the smooth & vacant course
that lacks abruption, one wave
the clinical mania un-
differentiated whiteness
contains when cylindrical cloud
hard & plastic comes to represent
the mind to the mind
& thus describe a model
of terrible momentum
with unity of purpose
toward nothing so much
as cold, radiant nature
stripped of Eros, of becoming,
just the mainframe

& its withering severity
without any predicate
of others, save perhaps their
gazes, no walls,
no nothing, completely
white light & your name
when your consciousness was
splitting time was stopping
you were going always into that.
I was going always to the mall
in those months,
the young century's rainiest
April & May, to walk the
baby & to understand my art.
I didn't understand.
I would move the stroller
through the halogen, over
grooved tile & across those
smooth marble expanses meant
to simulate floating & gliding
before that pure frictionless
feeling was entire. Sometimes
we'd go inside the stores.
Sears was still enormous
& because of its design
implied a bound series of
discrete, related worlds
linked by passages threatened
& precarious to me.
The connections felt
besieged or like a mask
for separation, they felt
like connection between us
in life but I didn't

take my allegory
further Krystle Cole, into your
lysergic delirium later redeemed
by a beautiful discipline
of spirit & cosmography
developed for praxis. I liked
your video on candy
flipping hard & developing
esp with friends.
It suggested oneness
was a leavened mix
of random indiscretion,
bruising wariness, & bliss
obtained by synchronizing
chemical encounter. Krystle,
there's a made up drug
I wonder if you'd do it?
Bradley Cooper, in *Limitless*
takes this little pill, which,
in its candy dot translucence
looks a lot like a tear plucked
from the cheek in Man Ray's "Larmes."
With it, he can utilize
all of his brain, & so
he un-riddles the patterning
hidden in the ceaseless
flow of capital, structuring its
chaos in excess of any mortal
with a terrible momentum
& unity of purpose toward
nothing so much as pure profit
& complete subordination
of the world. At the mall
certain spots sold old stuff: sports

memorabilia & video
games, vintage organs & deluxe
baby grands. In one store
there were highly priced
comics with toys & ephemera
related to the stories.
They had action figures
based on some series I guess
called *The Crisis of
Infinite Earths*. I wrote
the phrase down in my notebook
& realized only later that I'd
made a rather telling trans-
position, putting the word
'world' where 'earth' was & thinking
The Crisis of Infinite Worlds
I guess because anyone will
occasion *the* world as *a*
world its commonality precarious
but real, & the person
beside them does the same the person
far in every way from them will as well
where the wound of even
being in material conditions
where consciousness is made these
confrontations & arrangements
each taking their referent
then as earth or taking
something else entirely
as world—the word is profligate
& dense & transparent & cheap
& impossibly one the clearest pill.
In our minds it floods with light & we
see through that, life's benevolent corruption

in a radiance we can't make
any sense of. Krystle, have you ever,
just standing around,
noticed someone smoking
in an older silver Volvo
& watched the comeback feelings
of a Tupac Easter Sunday
steep in their ambivalent features
until they are more radiant
than cinematic virgins
having lost it in the wake
of Saint Maria Goretti
whose patronage is lost
to the brutalized sweetness
of her charges
when depicted in the mind
& reconstructed
as a low-res simulation
by scientists the weekend
Wall Street's occupied & particles
are found to go
faster than light
then weirdly feel like
this is paradise
not for *people*
but paradise
regardless.
That same May
I had gone to Detroit. I saw
the most wonderful graffiti, more
a prayer, written on a wall
in magic marker, it read—
Two Things:
   1) That we would grow closer & closer as time progresses.

2) That our ships would not crash.
Magic marker on a
surface doesn't have
much depth of skin.
You move it smoothly
on the wall & it stays smooth
barely records the softest friction
of two separate textures meeting.
The wetness of its onyx
dries quick or even quicker
if you blow on it with circled lips,
like clouds in old maps
that blew ships across a flat earth
to an edge I don't exactly
not idealize. That somewhere
there's a precipice in this world & tracing
my finger along those ardent lines
I'd found the fault of it
a little, in its boldness far too faint
& not enough.

LUCY'S STUDIO

I began writing *Lucy 72* at an artist colony where I spent much of the month drafting seventy-two poems written in long, loosely structured couplets that helped to address my thinking through the initial work. These poems, now honed down, but still in couplets, reveal a fluid narrative perspective that explores race, sexuality, and representation both within the field of my imagination and, simultaneously, in my observations and analyses of my experiences in the artists' colony in which these poems were written—as well as in others—where this exploration becomes further complicated and enriched.

When I attend most artist residencies, I am usually the "only one" by many criteria, often the only attending African American, certainly the only African-Filipino American. Add to this Queer, and add to that, I am often one of a few, or the only full-time academic cultural critic. And then add that I work as a multimedia artist in painting, video, sound, dance, and performance art. By all measures, I am usually an anomaly in these mostly, or all, white, straight, and traditionally single-medium centered artist colonies.

It is a challenging experience to thrive in these environments, as the "only one," subtly or not so subtly attacked with various degrees of intention and frequency. At a recent residency, during dinner, it was suggested that I be "strangled" for describing the super-thin, wealthy, post-plastic-surgery white women in a nearby neighborhood as somehow longing to vanish. Later, I was called an "asshole" for naming an art colonist's entitlement and white privilege in bypassing the colony's bureaucracy in claiming the largest, nicest room of our house that was not intended for her, simply because she felt it was. Another night, after sharing my experiences and ideas with some visiting artists about creating artwork in public environments, restaurants, bars, airport lounges, etc., I was informed that if I tried to do this in the major city where they lived, I would be "shut down," and that I "talk a big game." Clearly, I couldn't be telling the truth, and besides, *Who do I think I am?*

To be an anomaly creates drama, reveals risks, and opens possibilities. Lucy, via her poetic personae, speaks *outside* of her perceived race, or is *complicit in* her race as a white woman, a white woman who is also a fat brown young man, or not black, or shapes, sometimes becoming a flash of light, meditating on people, rocks, playing in rivers, skies, staring into beige walls, fans, or low grass.

Part imaginative landscape and real field report, the poems in *Lucy 72* expand around the core of what it might mean to be "the only one," to not be shut down, but to open up into reflection, to evade strangling, and to breathe. I attempt to capture the person, beyond name-calling, who speaks *through* race, sexuality, and representation, circulating in and out of the spaces where Lucy lives, and where we do too.

7. LUCY IS WHITE

My freedom is not white. Though my body is, I think, peach,
The color of what might be the insides of some animals.

There's melanin in me, deep in my fingers, the digits held not by shadow,
but like in my calves, darker, in summer, like in my house, erect.

In this, I am alive. Even at the risk of cancer, I step out in the sun. Even after flesh
cut and a mole pulled out, even after the tests, the results, I can only imagine tan.

In the sun, I am reminded I am human, that my body is whole. I am free to break
near the edge of whatever it is I want, say, to notice bikes collecting at a door.

Knowing is becoming the source, a familiar sign, not my peering out of a bush.
And I will not wash a dish.

In fact, I refuse to wait near any obligation, because I might leap off and dive
into a psychic grid of that which is familiar. I am blank, clear. I am pure, tested.

Last night, near the edge of a sea, there I was, lying yet arched up into the moon,
which looked heavy against the sky. It was yellow and cut the fog.

Or clouds. Like the hole in the needle in the haystack, I fit in, but I will not jump
from a hay bail. I do not think that I work like that.

Above me a roof, where water slides down, but I have no nation. I have no feeling
for boundary beyond my own.

I am playing a game. Can you guess it? My knees are bent and I pull something back.
It is winding backwards, wrapping around me.

8. LUCY RESPONDS TO MOTION AND REFLECTION

When the NORTH COUNTRY LINE SERVICE backs its truck below my window,
blaring Faith, the thunder outside no longer matters.

The towels wave in front of my window. I can see them flying by the white skin
of the driver, who I want.

What I love is that he could care less about the music that disrupts my writing.
He could care less about the blare of my fan, or the thunder as he throws towels.

Each one reminds me I am surrounded by whiteness, that my real body is not white,
and my mind longs for something outside of its sanctity.

This reveals itself in the white streaks that gather at the edges of my skull,
the features of my face, above my laptop which my hair covers.

I've decided to feel invisible for the day, to ignore the great back muscle that rips down his
back. I'm not here to think about that.

I'm here to leave a message, to deliver myself from my reflection, shadow and force.
What I did not capture is a flash near the water.

The rain stopped. I recognized a pair of jeans on a line. I don't question my looking
at the white paint on the house railing.

If I am taller, or thinner, or finer—If I am more wealthy than the next—If I can recline
or walk along a beach, surf or run, or sew—or if I have an important name.

I want to devoid myself of all but jaw, apple, and glance. For my need: linens, hurled
bag after bag into the big truck, he carries a single blue one back.

9. LUCY AND REDEMPTION

In another part of my being, I thought about what the bag meant. I couldn't think of it without the hurling motion of towels that flew by.

I felt that what contained my own whiteness was being a body not black. It's like I'm in a black people movie, when I stuff my face. You know, all fried food.

I am white, pure as the matter of paint that I painted at the borders of my room, pure as the coatings that lay thick on my walls.

One of my favorite words is *alabaster*. It suits me in the winter, when my blush lights up a room, the glasses stop their clinking, and I become less cold.

I hope that my sense is tied to my actions. If I address a black face with a smile, what will that face do? If I presuppose his or her color stable, will I rotate or fade?

I cannot lie. I'm not sure what I want from this existence. If only I were more real, instead of less brimming at the surface.

The feeling is like a film in the back of my mind. There's race. There's gender. There is my skin, decision and circumstance, which I hope to peel.

There is the real peeling that I pick from my back. I can't wait to run or to swim. No objects that I can see for any real sense of duration. The landscape shifts.

I concoct one sense of my self in one way, and then another way until I have no race. Really? Is my whiteness connected to a past beyond its own right?

When my body spins in the morning, I give it power. When I enter a room to sit down with such alert intelligence, of course, I have such stunning bones and hair.

My fork is not a weapon. At times, I think about spitting in people's faces, right while they are speaking to me. The spit flies from my mind, again and again.

13. LUCY, THE RAIN

When it starts and the pavement turns black, you will see me looking
for difference between what's dry and what shines.

Wetter than wet, beyond black, my whiteness is like my voice,
a melody of sunflowers bleached and dried in a closet.

I've never heard my voice beyond what I can only intuit—it sounds
girl enough for one to want to possess it, boy enough to trump the rain.

Sometimes, when it comes down, the drops crash on the pavement,
little explosions, the clarity of my speech.

I do not stutter, or vary my pitch. I do not smoke, or drink more than red.
Cropped pants: the sun runs. The field of flowers that grew,

I have picked clear. Next to a sea, I saw a pair of eyes, almost blue-green,
after which I lay out before the storm to rest.

Against my arm, a silver chair, and if I had a song to sing, it would begin
with my body, blocked. The day breaks out the darkening sky,

and when I wear black, I look even longer, my kick underneath even firmer,
they, too, say I light up a room, and they say, even my eyes are so clear.

17. LUCY AND FREEDOM

If I think about my own unwinding, I can see my freedom
in relation to the bug flicked

in the street, its wings soft from dying in the envelope.
In the night, its color, then, against the white of my room,

bouncing against the walls, brown and quick. I'm not sure if
its kind matters, smacking against the ceiling, to escape hardness.

I thought about it charging my body, its speed, and ruining
the neon bulb. Tricky spinner, I thought the noise I could deal with,

but the point when I realized I was done, it fell in my bed.
It didn't want to be caught, but it had to be captured.

The towel worked. Snapped in the air, trapped in a grey cap
filled with foam—

Below the flap—more tape—sealed. I'm not sure why I decided
to bake it over the bulb, maybe because of all the scratching.

There is a body inside of a body. I did not think of that then,
but I think of it now.

Several mirrors and revolving doors away, some blue planet shades into our sky. Intoxicated by this, as if by its own clairvoyance, the poem displays its plastic powers—fluoresces and, over time, decays. Still a transient and delicate substance, language nevertheless secures for us a strong interior, sharpness against our natural world. Of course, its occult successes in this regard must meet an equal measure of unsuccess: such that the leafy dark in the Courbet retain its phatic life, and the crisscross of rubble in Egypt not beautiful to the point of transparency or terror. Sometimes, a poem is made to furnish restlessness. Here, no longer romantic about its romanticism, the poem enters a satanic phase: dissatisfaction. Only fraudulence seems to make claims for truth, severe posturing, repetition, pain. The poem begins to take illusion seriously. It is not reflective, but lends passage to the unknown, generating visions, seizure, or deeper sleep. Technology develops to record the spectre of idea. Since we cannot face ourselves, self-denial acquires punishing power, pales in tempo, and draws sensation down. Not poorer for it, somehow, a fuller face appears. Do you hear it? The solitary body in the idleness of a painterly storm. This hallucination that something could be heard, beyond the vicissitudes of meaning. Today it is still not clear what the poem wants. Determination to give poetry the highest value... renders the poet absurd. And yet, for whatever reason, a certain density remains... a hesitation which refuses to toss this brightness to the wind.

ENEMY OF THE ABSOLUTE

I

Whose attending spirit holds me thus?

Whose shape-shifting wood

Thus tooled what

Kind of stew or meanness so

Sweetest sigh, a sudden face, a cliff that wears my

Own steps in

Darkness hush

Of words be beggarly, be master and native

To the gleaming glade.

II

Bright crowns and hills that wreathe

The innards of the nightingale.

A laugh whose inner bark

Scrapes against the olive leaves, dark green

And gray green, citations of aloha,

Movements of the cross.

From the outside

We are all tormented, jangling our bracelets

From heaven, its rural scent of knowing

What acts are now before us.

III

The Mexico we are still young from

Faking our own deaths

As children, shaking our futures

Before your eyes—

How warm the night is

With these feelings you've been avoiding.

The summer we spent in Oaxaca

Is at the same time inconceivable

And without eternity.

IV

For they teach us that eternity is

Not always where the mind is, nor held in judgment

By its furnishings, a beautiful sunset

Of human spirit.

Humid night.

Hamburger in mind, mind

White towel of imagery.

Weapons that turn outward to connect

With the harmony of things come not now

From the mind.

V

Perfect blue of the galaxy.

Stars that paddle across our eyes, across the yogurt and dream

Of the Persian Gulf

Have no gunmen to the fault.

Nor in the prehensile television of our minds

To retrace what we've killed, playing

Tricks on the dead.

Upward angel

Downward fish.

My face

Alone, and the sky.

THE POETS

ROSA ALCALÁ is the author of two books of poetry, *Undocumentaries* (Shearsman Books, 2010) and *The Lust of Unsentimental Waters* (Shearsman Books, 2012). *Spit Temple: The Selected Performances of Cecilia Vicuña* (Ugly Duckling Presse, 2012), which she edited, translated, and transcribed, was runner-up for the 2013 PEN Award for Poetry in Translation. She has also translated the work of Lila Zemborain, Lourdes Vázquez, and other poets, with translations included in *The Oxford Book of Latin American Poetry*. She is an associate professor in the Department of Creative Writing and Bilingual MFA at the University of Texas at El Paso.

ERIC BAUS is the author of *The To Sound* (Wave Books / Verse Press, 2004), *Tuned Droves* (Octopus Books, 2008), *Scared Text* (Colorado State University Press, 2011), and *The Tranquilized Tongue* (City Lights Publishing, 2014). His series of commentaries on poetry audio recordings, *Notes on PennSound*, was recently published in *Jacket2*. He lives in Denver.

ANSELM BERRIGAN's publications include *Notes from Irrelevance* (Wave Books, 2011); *Free Cell* (City Lights Publishing, 2009); *Skasers*, with John Coletti (Flowers & Cream Press, 2012); *Loading*, with artist Jonathan Allen (Brooklyn Arts Press, 2013); *Sure Shot* (Overpass Books, 2013); and *Zero Star Hotel* (Edge Books, 2002). A book-length poem, *Primitive State*, is due out in 2014 from Edge Books. He is a gratis editor and publisher, a part-time teacher and tutor, and a more or less protean fuckup of a kind.

EDMUND BERRIGAN is the author of two books of poetry, *Disarming Matter* (The Owl Press, 1999) and *Glad Stone Children* (Farfalla Press, 2008); and a quasi-memoir, *Can It!* (Letter Machine Editions, 2013). He is editor of *The Selected Poems of Steve Carey* (Subpress, 2009), and is co-editor with Anselm Berrigan and Alice Notley of *The Collected Poems of Ted Berrigan* (University of California Press, 2007) and *The Selected Poems of Ted Berrigan* (University of California Press, 2011). He is an editor for poetry magazines *Vlak* and *Brawling Pigeon*, and is on the editorial board of *Lungfull!* He lives in Brooklyn.

SUSAN BRIANTE is the author of *Pioneers in the Study of Motion* (Ahsahta Press, 2007) and *Utopia Minus* (Ahsahta Press, 2011). She is an associate professor of creative writing at the University of Arizona.

SOMMER BROWNING is the author of *Either Way I'm Celebrating* (Birds, LLC; 2011), a collection of poetry and comics, and a few chapbooks, most recently *The Presidents (and Other Jokes)* (Future Tense Books, 2013). She works as a librarian and lives with poet Noah Eli Gordon and their daughter.

JULIE CARR is the author of five books of poetry, including *100 Notes on Violence* (Ahsahta Press, 2010), *Sarah – Of Fragments and Lines* (Coffee House Press, 2010), and *RAG* (Omnidawn, 2014). *Surface Tension: Ruptural Time and the Poetics of Desire in Late Victorian Poetry*, was published by Dalkey Archive in 2013. She teaches at the University of Colorado in Boulder and is the co-publisher of Counterpath Press.

DON MEE CHOI is the author of *The Morning News Is Exciting* (Action Books, 2010) and the recipient of a 2011 Whiting Writers' Award. She is also a translator of contemporary Korean writing, including, most recently, Kim Hyesoon's *Princess Abandoned* (Tinfish Press, 2012) and *All the Garbage of the World Unite!* (Action Books, 2011), winner of the 2012 Lucien Stryk Asian Translation Prize.

ARDA COLLINS is the author of a collection of poems, *It Is Daylight* (Yale University Press, 2009), which was awarded the Yale Series of Younger Poets Prize. She is a recipient of the May Sarton Award from the American Academy of Arts and Sciences and holds a Ph.D. from the University of Denver. She has taught at the University of Iowa Writers' Workshop; the University of Massachussetts, Amherst; and most recently at NYU.

DOT DEVOTA is from a family of ranchers and rodeo stars. She is the author of *The Eternal Wall* (Cannibal Books, 2011; Canadian edition from BookThug, 2013), *MW: A Midwest Field Guide* (Editions19\, 2012), and *And the Girls Worried Terribly* (Noemi Press, 2014). She currently writes prose about the Midwest and travels full time.

TSERING WANGMO DHOMPA is the author of three collections of poetry: *My rice tastes like the lake* (Apogee Press, 2011), *In the Absent Everyday* (Apogee Press, 2005), and *Rules of the House* (Apogee Press, 2002). Her most recent work is a nonfiction book, *A Home in Tibet* (Penguin Books India, 2013). Dhompa was raised in the exiled Tibetan communities in India and Nepal. She lives in San Francisco and is pursuing a Ph.D. in literature at the University of California, Santa Cruz.

GRAHAM FOUST is the author of five books of poems, including *To Anacreon in Heaven and Other Poems* (Flood Editions, 2013). With Samuel Frederick, he is the translator of Ernst Meister's *In Time's Rift* (Wave Books, 2012). He teaches at the University of Denver.

C.S. GISCOMBE was born in Dayton, Ohio. His poetry books include *Prairie Style* (Dalkey Archive, 2008) and *Giscome Road* (Dalkey Archive, 1998); his prose books are *Into and Out of Dislocation* (North Point Press, 2000), *Ohio Railroads* (Omnidawn, 2014), and *Back Burner* (Dalkey Archive, 2015). He lives in Berkeley and teaches English at the University of California, Berkeley.

RENEE GLADMAN's writings and drawings explore language and narration as gestures of thought. Her most recent publication is *Ana Patova Crosses a Bridge* (Dorothy Publishing, 2013), the third installment of the Ravicka novella series. She lives and teaches in Providence, R.I., and runs Leon Works, an independent press for fiction, poetry, and the thinking text.

NOAH ELI GORDON is an assistant professor in the MFA program in creative writing at the University of Colorado-Boulder, where he currently directs Subito Press. His recent books include *The Year of the Rooster* (Ahsahta Press, 2013), *The Source* (Futurepoem Books, 2011), and *Novel Pictorial Noise* (Harper Perennial, 2007).

YONA HARVEY is a literary artist residing in Pittsburgh. She is the author of the poetry collection *Hemming the Water* (Four Way Books, 2013).

MATTHEW HENRIKSEN is the author of *Ordinary Sun* (Black Ocean, 2011) and the chapbooks *Another Word* (DoubleCrossed Press, 2009) and *Is Holy* (horse less press, 2006). He co-edits the online poetry journal *Typo*; sporadically publishes *Cannibal*, a hand-bound literary journal; and runs The Burning Chair Readings. He lives in the Arkansas Ozarks and works at Dickson Street Bookshop.

HARMONY HOLIDAY is a writer/archivist/choreographer/antiquefuturist living in New York. She is the author of *Negro League Baseball* (Fence Books, 2011) and *Go Find Your Father / A Famous Blues* (Gold Line Press, 2014). She is the founder of Afrosonics, a growing archive of rare jazz and poetry LPs.

CATHY PARK HONG's books of poetry include *Translating Mo'um* (Hanging Loose Press, 2002); *Dance Dance Revolution* (W.W. Norton, 2007), winner of the Barnard Women Poets Prize; and *Engine Empire* (W.W. Norton, 2012). Hong is also the recipient of a Fulbright Fellowship and a National Endowment for the Arts Fellowship. She is an associate professor at Sarah Lawrence College.

BHANU KAPIL teaches through the monster, memory, and experimental prose at Naropa University's Jack Kerouac School of Disembodied Poetics in Boulder, Colo. She is the author of five staged works, with accompanying performances in various parts of the world. Her most recent book is *Ban en Banlieue* (Nightboat Books, 2014).

JOHN KEENE is the author of *Annotations* (New Directions, 1995) and, with artist Christopher Stackhouse, of *Seismosis* (1913 Press, 2006). He is the translator of Brazilian author Hilda Hilst's *Letters from a Seducer* (Nightboat Books / A Bolha Editor, 2014). He has published fiction, poetry, essays, and translations widely, and his honors include a 2005 Whiting Foundation Fellowship in poetry and fiction. He teaches at Rutgers University in Newark, N.J.

AARON KUNIN is the author of two books of poems, *Folding Ruler Star* (Fence Books, 2005) and *The Sore Throat & Other Poems* (Fence Books, 2010). He has also written a novel, *The Mandarin* (Fence Books, 2008), and a book of aphorisms, sketches, and fragments, *Grace Period: Notebooks, 1998-2007* (Letter Machine Editions, 2013). An associate professor of English at Pomona College, he studies poetics, specializing in Renaissance literature. He lives in Los Angeles.

DOROTHEA LASKY is the author of *Thunderbird* (Wave Books, 2012), *Black Life* (Wave Books, 2010), and *AWE* (Wave Books, 2007). She is co-editor of *Open the Door: How To Excite Young People About Poetry* (McSweeney's Books, 2013). She is an assistant professor of poetry at Columbia University's School of the Arts and lives in New York City.

JULIANA LESLIE is the author of two books, *More Radiant Signal* (Letter Machine Editions, 2010) and *Green Is for World* (Coffee House Press, 2012), which was a 2011 National Poetry Series selection. She currently lives in Santa Cruz, Calif.

RACHEL LEVITSKY began writing poetry at age 31 after a short first life of activism. She went to get an MFA at Naropa University for help with the new system. Starting Belladonna Series helped her pull her two half-lives together. Her latest publication is the novel *The Story of My Accident Is Ours* (Futurepoem Books, 2013).

TAN LIN is the author of more than ten books, most recently, *Heath Course Pak* (Counterpath Press, 2012), *Bib. Rev. Ed* (Westphalie Verlag, 2011), *Insomnia and the Aunt* (Kenning Editions, 2011), and *7 Controlled Vocabularies and Obituary 2004 The Joy of Cooking* (Wesleyan, 2010). He is the recipient of a 2012 Foundation for Contemporary Arts Grant, a Getty Distinguished Scholar Grant, and a Warhol Foundation / Creative Capital Arts Writing Grant to complete a book on the writings of Andy Warhol. He is working on a sampled novel, *Our Feelings Were Made By Hand*. He is a professor of English and creative writing at New Jersey City University.

DAWN LUNDY MARTIN is the author of *A Gathering of Matter / A Matter of Gathering* (University of Georgia Press, 2007), winner of the Cave Canem Prize; *DISCIPLINE* (Nightboat Books, 2011), selected by Fanny Howe for the Nightbook Books Poetry Prize; *Candy*, a limited-edition chapbook (Albion Books, 2011); and *The Morning Hour* (Poetry Society of America, 2003). Her most recent book is *Life in a Box Is a Pretty Life* (Nightboat Books, 2014). She is a member of the experimental black poetry and performance group Black Took Collective and is an associate professor of English at the University of Pittsburgh.

J. MICHAEL MARTINEZ's first book, *Heredities* (LSU Press, 2010), won the Walt Whitman Award from The Academy of American Poets. His second book is *In The Garden of the Bridehouse* (University of Arizona Press, 2014).

FARID MATUK is the author of *This Isa Nice Neighborhood* (Letter Machine Editions, 2010) and *My Daughter La Chola* (Ahsahta Press, 2013). He serves as contributing editor for *The Volta*, poetry editor for *Fence*, and teaches in the MFA program at the University of Arizona.

SHANE McCRAE is the author of *Mule* (Cleveland State University Poetry Center, 2010), *Blood* (Noemi Press, 2013), and three chapbooks—most recently, *Nonfiction* (Black Lawrence Press, 2014), winner of the Black River Chapbook Competition. He has received a Whiting Writers' Award and a fellowship from the National Endowment for the Arts. He teaches in the brief-residency MFA program at Spalding University.

ANNA MOSCHOVAKIS's recent books are *You and Three Others Are Approaching a Lake* (Coffee House Press, 2011) and a translation of *The Jokers* by Egyptian-French novelist Albert Cossery (New York Review Books Classics, 2010). She teaches at Pratt Institute and Milton Avery Graduate School of the Arts at Bard, and is a member of Brooklyn-based publishing collective Ugly Duckling Presse.

FRED MOTEN is author of *In the Break: The Aesthetics of the Black Radical Tradition* (University of Minnesota Press, 2003); *Hughson's Tavern* (Leon Works, 2008); *B. Jenkins* (Duke University Press, 2010); *The Undercommons: Fugitive Planning and Black Study*, with Stefano Harney (Autonomedia, 2013); *The Feel Trio* (Letter Machine Editions, 2014); and *consent not to be a single being* (Duke University Press, forthcoming). He lives in Los Angeles and teaches at the University of California, Riverside.

SAWAKO NAKAYASU writes and translates poetry, and her recent book, *Mouth: Eats Color—Sagawa Chika Translations, Anti-Translations, & Originals* (Rogue Factorial, 2011) does both in one work. Other recent books include *Texture Notes* (Letter Machine Editions, 2010) and *Hurry Home Honey* (Burning Deck, 2009), and books of translation include Ayane Kawata's *Time of Sky & Castles in the Air* (Litmus Press, 2010) and Takashi Hiraide's *For the Fighting Spirit of the Walnut* (New Directions, 2008), which received the Best Translated Book Award in 2009.

CHRIS NEALON teaches in the English Department at Johns Hopkins University. He is the author of two books of poetry, *The Joyous Age* (Black Square Editions, 2004), and *Plummet* (Edge Books, 2009), as well as a chapbook, *The Dial* (The Song Cave, 2012). He has also written two books of literary criticism: *Foundlings: Lesbian and Gay Historical Emotion Before Stonewall* (Duke University Press, 2001), and *The Matter of Capital: Poetry and Crisis in the American Century* (Harvard University Press, 2011). He lives in Washington, D.C.

HOA NGUYEN is the author of eight books and chapbooks. She currently lives in Toronto where she teaches poetics in a private workshop and at Ryerson University. Her latest full-length collection of poems is *As Long As Trees Last* (Wave Books, 2012).

KHADIJAH QUEEN is the author of *Conduit* (Black Goat / Akashic Books, 2008) and *Black Peculiar* (Noemi Press, 2011), winner of the 2010 Noemi Press Book Award. Four times nominated for the Pushcart Prize, her poetry has appeared in the anthologies *Villanelles* (Random House, 2012), *Best American Nonrequired Reading* (Houghton Mifflin, 2010), and *Powder: Writing by Women in the Ranks from Vietnam to Iraq* (Kore Press, 2008). She is a Cave Canem fellow and visual artist and is currently working on an illustrated mixed-genre project.

ANDREA REXILIUS is the author of *Half of What They Carried Flew Away* (Letter Machine, 2012) and *To Be Human Is To Be a Conversation* (Rescue Press, 2011). She teaches at Naropa University's Jack Kerouac School of Disembodied Poetics, where she also coordinates the JKS Summer Writing Program. She is a member of the Poets' Theater group GASP (Girls Assembling Something Perpetual).

ZACHARY SCHOMBURG is the author of four books of poems, including most recently, *The Book of Joshua* (Black Ocean, 2014). He co-edits Octopus Books and co-curates the Bad Blood Reading Series in Portland, Ore.

BRANDON SHIMODA is the author of four books of poetry—*Portuguese* (Tin House Books, 2013), *O Bon* (Litmus Press, 2011), *The Girl Without Arms* (Black Ocean, 2011), and *The Alps* (Flim Forum Press, 2008)—as well as numerous limited editions of collaborations, drawings, writings, and songs. Born in California, he has lived since in eleven states and six countries, most recently Maine, Taiwan, and Tucson, Ariz.

EVIE SHOCKLEY is the author of four poetry collections—*the new black* (Wesleyan Press, 2012), winner of the 2012 Hurston/Wright Legacy Award in Poetry; *a half-red sea* (Carolina Wren Press, 2006); and two chapbooks— and a book of criticism, *Renegade Poetics: Black Aesthetics and Formal Innovation in African American Poetry* (University of Iowa Press, 2011). Her honors include the 2012 Holmes National Poetry Prize; fellowships from MacDowell, Millay Colony for the Arts, American Council of Learned Socities, and Schomburg Center for Research in Black Culture. She serves as creative editor on the editorial collective of *Feminist Studies*; from 2007-2011, she co-edited the journal *jubilat*. Shockley is associate professor of English at Rutgers University.

CEDAR SIGO was raised on the Suquamish Reservation in Washington state. He studied writing and poetics at Jack Kerouac School of Disembodied Poetics at Naropa University. His books include *Selected Writings* (Ugly Duckling Presse, 2003), *Stranger In Town* (City Lights Publishing, 2010), and *Language Arts* (Wave Books, 2014). He lives in San Francisco.

ABRAHAM SMITH hails from northwestern Wisconsin. His poetry collections are *Only Jesus Could Icefish in Summer* (Action Books, 2014); *Hank* (Action Books, 2010); and *Whim Man Mammon* (Action Books, 2007). His reading highlights include stints at the Academy of American Poets' Rooftop Reading Series and *Opium Magazine*'s

Literary Death Match. He is the recipient of fellowships from the Fine Arts Work Center and the Alabama State Council on the Arts. Presently, he is co-editing (with poet Shelly Taylor) *Hick Poetics* (Lost Roads Press, 2014), an anthology of countrified poet types. Smith is an instructor of English at University of Alabama.

CHRISTOPHER STACKHOUSE wrote the volume of poetry *Plural* (Counterpath Press, 2012). *Seismosis* (1913 Press, 2006) features Stackhouse's drawings in dialogue with text by John Keene. He is a visiting critic at Maryland Institute College of Art, Hoffberger School of Painting; guest lecturer at New York Center for Art & Media Studies; and visiting faculty at Naropa University's Summer Writing Program. With artists Jomar Statkun and Jared Friedman, he is founder of art and residency project This Red Door. Stackhouse is an advisory board member at *Fence*, contributing editor at *BOMB*, and contributing editor at *Vanitas*.

MATHIAS SVALINA is the author of four books, most recently *Wastoid* (Big Lucks, 2014) and *The Depression*, a collaboration with the photographer Jon Pack (Civil Coping Mechanisms, 2015). With Alisa Heinzman, Hajara Quinn, and Zachary Schomburg, he co-edits Octopus Books.

ROBERTO TEJADA is author of the poetry collections *Mirrors for Gold* (Krupskaya, 2006), *Exposition Park* (Wesleyan Press, 2010), and *Full Foreground* (University of Arizona Press, 2012). Founding editor of the journal *Mandorla: New Writing from the Americas*, he has translated work by poets José Lezama Lima, Eduardo Milán, María Baranda, and Alfonso D'Aquino. An art historian, Tejada's publications include *National Camera: Photography and Mexico's Image Environment* (University of Minnesota Press, 2009), *A Ver: Celia Alvarez Muñoz* (University of Minnesota Press, 2009), and the co-edited volume *Modern Art in Africa, Asia and Latin America: An Introduction to Global Modernisms* (Wiley-Blackwell, 2012). His work has earned awards from the Creative Capital / Warhol Foundation and the National Endowment for the Arts.

TC TOLBERT is a genderqueer, feminist poet, and teacher. Assistant director of Casa Libre en la Solana, instructor at University of Arizona and Pima Community College, and wilderness instructor at Outward Bound, s/he is the author of *Gephyromania* (Ahsahta Press, 2014) and chapbooks *spirare* (Belladonna*, 2012), and *territories of folding* (Kore Press, 2011). Tolbert is co-editor, along with Tim Trace Peterson, of *Troubling the Line: Trans and Genderqueer Poetry and Poetics* (Nightboat Books, 2013).

CATHERINE WAGNER's collections of poems include *Nervous Device* (City Lights Publishing, 2012) and three previous collections from Fence Books. She teaches in the MA program in creative writing at Miami University and lives in Oxford, Ohio, with her son.

DANA WARD is the author of *Some Other Deaths of Bas Jan Ader* (Flowers & Cream, 2013), *The Crisis of Infinite*

Worlds (Futurepoem Books, 2013), and *This Can't Be Life* (Edge Books, 2012). He lives in Cincinnati, Ohio, where he hosts the Cy Press Poetry @ Thunder Sky Reading Series, and edits, with Paul Coors, Perfect Lovers Press.

RONALDO V. WILSON is the author of *Narrative of the Life of the Brown Boy and the White Man* (University of Pittsburgh Press, 2008) and *Poems of the Black Object* (Futurepoem Books, 2009). He is currently an assistant professor of Literature at University of California, Santa Cruz.

LYNN XU is the author of *Debts & Lessons* (Omnidawn, 2013) and the chapbook *June* (Corollary Press, 2006). She is currently a Ph.D. candidate in Comparative Literature at University of California, Berkeley, and she co-edits Canarium Books. With her husband, poet Joshua Edwards, she lives in Marfa, Texas.

PERMISSIONS

ROSA ALCALÁ: "Voice Activation" and "Dear Stranger," first appeared in *Mandorla: New Writing from the Americas*; "Training" and "Missing" first appeared in *Eleven Eleven*; and "Archaeology of Vestments" first appeared in *inactual magazine*. All poems are copyright ©2013 by Rosa Alcalá. Reprinted by permission of the author.

ERIC BAUS: "Dear Birds, I'm running out of numbers.," "Dearest Sister, Sugar is suffering somewhere in water.," and "The sleeper develops in the chords of my throat." are from *The To Sound*. Copyright ©2004 by Eric Baus. Reprinted by permission of Wave Books / Verse Press and the author. "Inside Any Good Song Someone Is Lost" and "They Showed a Film of Me Walking to Water" are from *Tuned Droves*. Copyright ©2008 by Eric Baus. Reprinted by permission of Octopus Books and the author.

ANSELM BERRIGAN: Excerpt from *Notes from Irrelevance* is from *Notes from Irrelevance*. Copyright ©2011 by Anselm Berrigan. Reprinted by permission of Wave Books and the author.

EDMUND BERRIGAN: "Little pieces continue as pieces," "Some Ancestor of Mine," and "mom and dad in a photo" are reprinted by permission of the author. Copyright ©2013 by Edmund Berrigan. "Disturningly" is from *Glad Stone Children*. Copyright ©2008 by Edmund Berrigan. Reprinted by permission of Farfalla Press / McMillan & Parrish and the author. "For Robinson Jeffers" is from *Disarming Matter*. Copyright ©1999 by Edmund Berrigan. Reprinted by permission of The Owl Press and the author.

SUSAN BRIANTE: "Nail Guns in the Morning," "Alexander Litvinenko," "Isabella," and "Specimen Box" are from *Utopia Minus*. Copyright ©2011 by Susan Briante. Reprinted by permission of Ahsahta Press and the author.

SOMMER BROWNING: "The Whistler," "*from* Friend [Sommer, I'm dying]," and "Grillz & Roebuck" are copyright ©2013 by Sommer Browning. Reprinted by permission of the author. "Either Way I'm Celebrating" and "The Opposite of Love" are from *Either Way I'm Celebrating*. Copyright ©2011 by Sommer Browning. Reprinted by permission of Birds, LLC and the author.

JULIE CARR: "29," "32," and "35" are from *100 Notes on Violence*. Copyright ©2010 by Julie Carr. Reprinted by permission of Ahsahta Press and the author. "from *RAG* [The fact is, I never much liked him peonies bloom]" and "from *RAG* [I had no other alternative]" are from *RAG*. Copyright ©2013 by Julie Carr. Reprinted by permission of Omnidawn Publishing and the author.

the reality of my imperative need to truly understand the nature of all animal behavior," and "Mostly to uncover the reality of my ultrainterior cruelty" are from *Black Peculiar*. Copyright ©2011 by Khadijah Queen. Reprinted by permission of Noemi Press and the author.

ANDREA REXILIUS: "What is the emanation of their image?" and "This is the answer of their fourth crossing." are from *Half of What They Carried Flew Away*. Copyright ©2012 by Andrea Rexilius. Reprinted by permission of Letter Machine Editions and the author.

ZACHARY SCHOMBURG: "Invisible and Not Invisible" and "The Black Hole" are from *Scary, No Scary*. Copyright ©2009 by Zachary Schomburg. "Death Letter," "Someone Falls in Love with Someone," and "The Person Who Was Expected" are from *Fjords Vol. 1*. Copyright ©2012 by Zachary Schomburg. All poems reprinted by permission of Black Ocean and the author.

BRANDON SHIMODA: "from *Lake M & Evening Oracle*" is partially from *O Bon*. Copyright ©2011 by Brandon Shimoda. Reprinted by permission of Litmus Press and the author.

EVIE SHOCKLEY: "a dark scrawl," "legit-i-mate," "'the people want the regime to fall,'" "studies in antebellum literature, ch. 5 (or, topsy-turvy)," and "weather or not" are copyright ©2013 by Evie Shockley. Reprinted by permission of the author.

CEDAR SIGO: "Dream," "Ode," and "Paris" are from *Language Arts*. Copyright ©2014 by Cedar Sigo. Reprinted by permission of Wave Books and the author. "Simple Gift" is from *Stranger In Town*. Copyright ©2010 by Cedar Sigo. Reprinted by permission of City Lights Publishing and the author.

ABRAHAM SMITH: "IN THE OLD DAYS redwing blackbirds…" is copyright ©2013 by Abraham Smith. Reprinted by permission of the author.

CHRISTOPHER STACKHOUSE: "Angel Smoke," "The artists, they want to sit in a room together," and "Thought as Tuning Fork" are from *Plural*. Copyright ©2013 by Christopher Stackhouse. Reprinted by permission of Counterpath Press and the author. "2:49 pm" and "On the Precipice of Water" are copyright ©2013 by Christopher Stackhouse. Reprinted by permission of the author.

MATHIAS SVALINA: "The Wine-Dark Sea [I reach for the kerosene of stars.]," "The Wine-Dark Sea [In these holy days]," and "The Wine-Dark Sea [Two doors stand open]" are copyright ©2013 by Mathias Svalina. "The Wine-Dark Sea [I want to answer questions,]" first appeared in *The Volta* and "The Wine-Dark Sea [I am trying]" first appeared in *Gulf Coast*. Copyright ©2013 by Mathias Svalina. Reprinted by permission of the author.